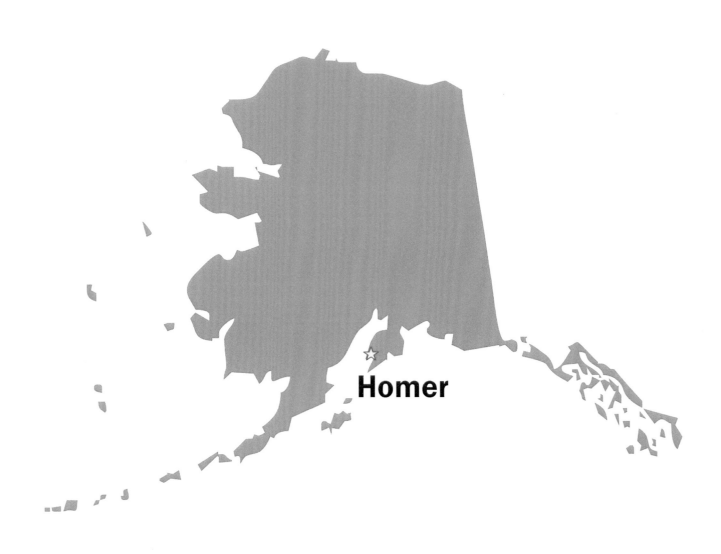

Homer

COSMIC KITCHEN; BREAKFAST, LUNCH AND FRIENDS

By Sean Hogan
and Michelle Wilson

Cosmic Kitchen; Breakfast, Lunch and Friends
ISBN 978-1-890692-34-6
© 2016, Sean Hogan and Michelle Wilson

Text by Sean Hogan

Main photography by Gary Sheridan, © Gary Sheridan, and Michelle Wilson, © Michelle Wilson

Additional photographs by Tim Steinberg, © Tim Steinberg; Paul Baylink, © Paul Baylink; Scott Dickerson, © Scott Dickerson; Alan Parks, © Alan Parks; Ian Reed, © Ian Reed.

Bumper stickers courtesy of Chris Etzwiler and Ginger and Denny Van Wagoner

Every effort has been made to contact copyright holders. The authors will be glad to correct any errors or omissions in future editions.

Cover Design: Dan Coe

Wizard Works
P.O. Box 1125
Homer, AK 99603

To Aileen & Hambone

for bringing us joy and happiness always

Table of Contents

IN THE BEGINNING...

When Cosmic Kitchen first opened its doors in May of 2003, it was the culmination of more than 13 years of travel and culinary experience gained at restaurants from Florida to California, Alaska to Arizona, Switzerland to Hawaii.

At last count, before opening our own business, I had worked in more than 40 restaurants, hotels, and catering companies. I believe it was a subconscious training for the inevitable step off the deep end into self employment. I'd cooked in Zurich, Switzerland (lots of Rosti), Asian food in Honolulu, Hawaii, French food, Mexican, Italian, Gourmet dinners in Palm Beach, and Cowboy lunches in Scottsdale, Arizona. The spark finally ignited in the winter of 2003 to open our own restaurant. So with a collection of great recipes, and years of experience, Michelle and I put together a business plan for the restaurant.

We came to Homer in a roundabout way, and that is a story in itself.

I grew up in Dublin, Ireland, attended UCD, and, like thousands of Irish students, went to the U.S. on Summer Work Visas. College isn't for everyone, and for me the stimulation of the work environment, versus the inertia of school, seemed more attractive.

Michelle and I crossed paths in Phoenix in 1985 and have been together ever since.

We moved to San Diego, where I got work at a busy little French restaurant called Café Chanticleer, owned by a Danish Chef, Erik Pedersen, and his wife, Marna. With practically no experience, and only two years of college science, it was challenging to meet Erik's expectations of culinary knowledge and taste. Even though hired as a dishwasher, I soon became his protégé, learning and developing skills that have served me to this day. Michelle helped out occasionally in Café Chanticleer also, and we still joke about Erik's martinet ways, akin to the "soup nazi", much beloved and feared, but with undeniable good taste.

Erik encouraged us to take on a second location of his, The Crown Bistro, in Coronado, CA. Michelle and I got our first taste of being entrepreneur restaurant managers. A highly popular and successful restaurant over the bridge from San Diego, we were very happy, but somehow wanderlust intervened, and I knew I needed to broaden my skills through travel, education, or both. And so we did.

Michelle and I first came to Homer in 1990 to visit her parents, who had been spending their winters in Florida. Aileen and Hambone, (his long-time nick-name) had been traveling up to Nikiski from Florida for years, and had told us lots of stories about their adventures in Alaska. So one year Michelle and I thought we'd take a trip up there also.

We bought a small travel trailer and truck, loaded up our belongings, and headed off from Florida, stopping along the way to visit with family and friends in Minnesota before picking up the Alcan Highway. Michelle read from The Milepost as we side tripped up the Cassiar Highway, pointing out the sites and history of different areas. Aileen and Hambone delighted in showing us around their summer home, and we took frequent day trips with them, even sightseeing in Ham's Cessna 180. A retired United Airlines Captain, Hambone shared Alaskans' love of flying, especially off gravel strips.

One day we drove down to Homer, and Michelle and I were wowed by the little town as we came down the hill, with its surrounding glaciers, moun-

tains, bays, and wide vistas. I fished at the Fishing Hole on the Spit, and Hambone took us to his favorite dive, being on first name basis with the waitress (as always!). We sensed this was somewhere we would return, and we did, the following summer. Again towing our little Jayco trailer behind us, loaded with bicycles and surfboards, we prepared to get jobs and work the season like all the other "spit rats" who make Homer their summer abode.

On Memorial Day weekend, we landed jobs with a local baker, who needed help for the busy summer season, and so we settled in to being summer locals — drinking at the Salty Dawg, fishing and actually catching salmon, and getting to know some of the colorful Homerites, such as Brother Asaiah, who would become significant later in our lives.

We headed back to Florida after that summer of work experience in Alaska. I had planned to attend

another great adventure, so we packed up, and headed off to the land of Aloha.

Florida Culinary Institute, and Michelle resumed her profession as a Dialysis Nurse.

Upon graduating Florida Culinary Institute, I took the opportunity to do a "Stagiaire" (apprenticeship) for a year at a Môvenpick Hotel just outside of Zurich, Switzerland. So Michelle and I headed off for the Grand Tour. She, not being eligible to work, played the good hostess, socializing with the other stagiaires, holding impromptu gatherings and fondue parties. She always says it was one of the best times of her life. Europe is nice, but now the U.S. was my home, and after a year, we were glad to be back in sunny South Florida, where we settled down in Juno Beach.

Well the road called again, and this time it was Hawaii. Somehow I talked Michelle into combining my culinary interests with my love of watersports (windsurfing back then, kitesurfing now) into

Little did we know that jobs were scarce, but Dialysis Nurses were in high demand, luckily for Michelle. I worked for Marriott Corporation at University of Hawaii, catering and preparing the Shintani Diet, a Hawaiian Native Foods diet plan. It was a great education in the polyglot culinary world of the Islands, with influences of Japanese, Chinese, Filipino, Korean, and Hawaiian styles all fused together, as are seen in the Cosmic Kitchen menu of today. And of course, the wind-surfing was excellent!

Though we loved Hawaii, Homer was calling, and the offer of summer work lured us back as surely as the shorebirds return every spring. And so we became summer visitors for a few years, wintering in Hawaii, just like our friends, the Golden Plovers.

I guess the nomadic years were coming to an end when we decided to "over-winter" in Homer. It seemed so fun in summer, winter couldn't be that bad, could it? So we settled down in 2001, Michelle taking a nursing position at the medical clinic, and I took a job at the natural food store. We learned to cross-country ski, skated on the frozen lakes, took yoga classes, and spent more time with friends. It all seemed right. Only one thing was missing...you know it...a good little restaurant!

My basic idea was to have a quick service, take-out Mexican joint, but then added burgers, sandwiches, salads, breakfast, espresso; the menu just kept growing. Eventually we got beer & wine, smoothies, shakes, catering menu, dinner menu, kid's menu, and foods catering to specific dietary needs. But back to the original

business plan...the Homer Chamber of Commerce helped us develop it to resemble a small volume manual on how to get bank financing, permits, and other invaluable information critical to opening your own business.

We found a location on Pioneer Avenue which seemed suitable, and signed the lease in February 2003. For gypsies like us, it was a nerve wracking time, but it seemed everyone was supportive and enthusiastic about our plans. We couldn't back out now and "hit the road", though it might have crossed our minds.

The upstairs apartment got renovated, the parking lot was expanded, and the whole building was redone with electrical wiring and plumbing up to code for the big day, May 1st. Equipment began arriving, new chairs, new tables, new floors, new lighting, even new walls, as it was an old building that wasn't even fully insulated. But the restaurant needed a name! So we began to debate what our idea represents. I liked "Kitchen" in the sense that it would suggest a closeness to the food, and the people preparing it. Michelle liked "Cosmic" as part of the name to reference our friend, Brother Asaiah, a Homer local who was very supportive of all community efforts and who coined the phrase "Cosmic Hamlet by the Sea" to refer to Homer. So finally the sign arrives and everything falls into place: Cosmic: /käzmik/ adj. of or relating to the universe or cosmos, especially as distinct from the earth, inconceivably vast, immense, colossal, prodigious, limitless.

We celebrated our 10 year anniversary May 1, 2013, with a party to show our appreciation to the town that welcomed us to such a wonderful home, and we would like to share these recipes with you, and with those who wish they were here in Homer right now. We wouldn't change a thing if we had to start all over again!

COSMIC BREAKFASTS

Breakfast

We evolved from being just a fast-food restaurant into a full-service one as we added items over the years – we got a beer and wine license, upgraded to a sophisticated point-of-sale ordering system, installed a commercial dishwasher and expanded the "back of the house." We started off just using paper plates and disposable utensils, but sensed our clientele preferred the full dining experience, with regular plates and silverware. Nowadays, all our takeout orders are packed in biodegradable boxes and include plastic-ware made of corn products. A large walk-in freezer allows us to order deliveries in bulk as food costs inevitably increase.

We are always looking for ways to improve, and recently expanded the "front of the house" with a heated, enclosed patio for year-round use.

We serve breakfast until 3 p.m. and it often peaks around 1 p.m., when regulars crave our huevos, eggs benny or big bang breakfast burrito smothered in enchilada sauce. For some reason, customers compulsively order the same item at breakfast, same drink, even at the same time of day. Some days the staff gets worried if the regulars don't show up — What happened, where's Bob? Have you seen Linda and Joan? Did Rita come in yet? It's Thursday — are we ready for Suzy and George? It's Friday – that's Margaret on the phone!

It's possible we serve the best _damn_ breakfast in town, if not even the whole state of Alaska.

Welcome to the Cosmic Kitchen.

HUEVOS RANCHEROS

This traditional Mexican breakfast of layered beans, eggs, tortillas and sauce is one of our most popular menu items. We serve it with crispy hash browns topped with cheese, sour cream and chorizo.

~ Makes enough for 2 ~

1 cup cooked Pinto Beans (pg. 99)
1 cup Enchilada Sauce (pg. 107)
4 (6-inch) corn tortillas
1 tablespoon butter
4 eggs
½ cup shredded Cheddar/Jack cheese
2 teaspoons sour cream

1. Pre-heat the beans and enchilada sauce in separate saucepans (or microwave).

2. Warm up the tortillas in a non-stick skillet, set them aside, stacked 2 per plate. Butter the pan lightly and fry the eggs, flipping them over easy, as we say in the restaurant lingo.

3. Layer the beans on top of the tortillas, topped with 2 eggs. Pour the enchilada sauce over the eggs and sprinkle the cheese on top. Melt cheese under a hot broiler (or microwave 10-15 seconds). Top with sour cream and enjoy.

FAJITA OMELET

We serve breakfast until 3 p.m. each day at CK and don't understand why most restaurants limit the time you can order eggs. This omelet is easy and delish and now you can make it anytime you want!

~ Makes enough for 2 ~

1 tablespoon butter
1 cup Fajita Veggies (pg. 115)
½ cup diced ham
4 eggs
1 cup shredded Cheddar/Jack cheese
½ cup Salsa Fresca (pg. 138)

1. Place a large nonstick frying pan over medium heat. Melt the butter in pan then add the veggies and ham; sauté for 2 to 3 minutes.

2. Beat the eggs with a fork in a small bowl.

3. Add the eggs to the pan, lifting the edges as it begins to set, allowing the liquid eggs to run underneath. When the mixture is almost dry, sprinkle ½ the cheese over it, fold over the omelet with a spatula and sprinkle remaining cheese on top. Remove pan from heat and cover for 1-2 minutes.

4. Cut omelet in half and top with salsa. Serve with toast.

CHORIZO SCRAMBLE

Michelle and I lived in San Diego for a number of years, where we came to love Mexican food, especially local dives that served authentic specialties such as Machaca (shredded beef) or Chorizo con huevos. After moving to Alaska, we still craved the flavors of Southern California and thought we should share them with Homer Alaskans. Chorizo is a piquant Mexican pork sausage; a great compliment to eggs and potatoes, and for filling burritos, tacos, quesadillas, etc.

Chorizo
2 tablespoons chili powder
1 teaspoon oregano
1 teaspoon cumin
½ teaspoon ground coriander
¼ teaspoon crushed red pepper
½ teaspoon salt
¼ teaspoon black pepper
2 cloves garlic, minced
1 pound ground pork
1 tablespoon apple cider vinegar

Chorizo Scramble
1 tablespoon butter
8 large eggs
1 cup shredded Cheddar/Jack cheese
12 corn tortillas
1 cup Salsa Fresca (pg. 138)
2 tablespoons sour cream

~ Makes enough for 4 ~

1. Mix all the dry spices in a bowl, then add the pork and vinegar. Using your hands, combine this mixture until thoroughly blended. Cover and refrigerate for a few hours (or overnight).
2. Preheat a large saucepan over medium heat, add Chorizo and stir frequently to avoid sticking, and cook to 165° F.
3. Melt the butter in a large nonstick pan and scramble the eggs. Fold in Chorizo and shredded cheese and remove from heat.
4. Serve with warmed tortillas, salsa and sour cream.

* Hint: Cosmic secret – add a teaspoon of jalapeño juice from the jar into your sour cream tub for zestier tang.

SPINACH SCRAMBLE

We pulled our travel-trailer into Homer on Memorial Day weekend 1991 and by Friday afternoon we had gotten our first jobs in town at the Fresh Sourdough Express Bakery. A venerable Homer institution, the "Dough" was owned by Kevin and Donna Maltz, emphasizing local and organic products. We fell in love with Homer that summer, camping on the Spit, fishing at the "fishing hole", 18 hours of daylight and the friendly, quirkiness of local characters such as Brother Asaiah, Spoon Mike, Jean the Eagle Lady and the Kilchers. We vowed to return someday but it wouldn't be for another 8 years. So next time you're in town, pick up a loaf of Sourdough, wish aloha to Donna and Kevin, and toast the bread while preparing this easy recipe.

~ Makes enough for 2 ~

2 tablespoons butter
½ cup onions, diced
2 cups fresh spinach
6 large eggs (beaten in bowl)
½ cup shredded Cheddar/Jack cheese
2 tablespoons feta cheese
salt and pepper to taste
1 tablespoon sour cream

1. Heat 1 tablespoon of butter in a medium size nonstick fry pan; add the onions and spinach and cook until the spinach is wilted, then set aside in a bowl. Wipe out the hot pan and continue using it.
2. Melt 1 tablespoon butter in pan again, pour eggs into it and scramble lightly.
3. As the eggs begin to dry up add the spinach, Cheddar/Jack and feta, and season with salt and pepper.
4. Top with sour cream and serve with crispy home fries and Sourdough toast.

BIG BANG
BREAKFAST BURRITO

Cosmic Kitchen is famous for Big Burritos that'll fill you up for a hard day of Alaska living, sightseeing or fishing. We seem to be the place where people stop in when they first arrive in town and also to pick up a burrito for the road trip out of town.

It all started with a Big Bang and it feels like we've made billions and billions of 'em!

~ Makes one Burrito ~

1 teaspoon canola oil
⅓ cup Fajita Veggies (pg. 115)
½ cup Cosmic Redskin Potatoes (pg. 21)
2 large eggs
⅓ cup cooked and diced sausage, bacon or ham
½ cup shredded Cheddar/Jack cheese
¼ cup Salsa Fresca (pg. 138)
1 large flour tortilla
½ cup Enchilada Sauce (pg. 107)

1. In a medium nonstick pan heat the oil over medium heat. Add the veggies and potatoes and sauté for 4 to 5 minutes.
2. Push this mixture aside, then scramble the eggs in the same pan.
3. Add in the cooked breakfast meat and stir everything together, topping with ¼ cup of shredded cheese and salsa.
4. Place the tortilla on top of this to warm up and melt the cheese.
5. Put the tortilla on a large plate and spread the mixture on top, fold the sides of the tortilla over the filling – left and right – then roll up Jellyroll like, with the seam side down.
6. Top with enchilada sauce and rest of cheese – broil or microwave for 12 minutes and serve piping hot.

EGGS BENEDICT

It's still a favorite, and customers rave about our hollandaise. Of course, we use real butter and the secret is adding a little cayenne and lemon juice at the end.

~ Makes 4 servings ~

2 cups unsalted butter
4 egg yolks
1 tablespoon red wine vinegar
⅛ teaspoon cayenne pepper
1 tablespoon lemon juice
4 English muffins
8 slices Canadian bacon (or ham)
8 poached eggs

1. Melt 2 cups of butter in a 2 quart saucepan over medium heat, and allow to cool slightly.
2. In a medium size pot bring 2 cups of water to a simmer and rest a heatproof bowl over the pot. Add the egg yolks and vinegar to the bowl, whisking for 2-3 minutes. Remove the bowl from pot and add the melted butter in a steady stream, whisking constantly for 2-3 minutes until a lightly thickened sauce is formed. Finish off by whisking in the cayenne and lemon juice.
3. Toast the English muffins and fry the Canadian bacon in a pan.
4. Poach the eggs in a pot of boiling water (add a little white vinegar to the water as it helps to coagulate the egg whites) for 3-4 minutes. Place the Canadian bacon on top of each half of English muffin and top off with a poached egg. Spoon hollandaise over the eggs and serve with homestyle potatoes or hash browns.

SMOKY BAY QUICHE

"If you're not capable of a little sorcery, you shouldn't bother cooking."

Sidonie-Gabrielle Colette

Our first winter in Homer, I worked at Smoky Bay Natural Food Store and Michelle (a registered nurse by profession) worked at Homer Medical Clinic. Carol Standaert was the excellent chef at Smoky Bay and we collaborated on creative ways to use up the previous week's delivery of organic produce and exotic cheeses. That store eventually closed down, but some of the great recipes live on and make "special" appearances at Cosmic Kitchen, such as this one for Quiche. Get creative and throw in any extra cheese you have on hand (feta, Swiss, etc.) and other cooked veggie leftovers such as broccoli, potatoes or squash.

~ Makes 6-8 servings ~

Crust
4 ounces (1 stick) butter
1 cup flour
¼ cup grated parmesan cheese
3-4 tablespoons cold water

1. Cut the butter into cubes and place in a food processor with the flour and parmesan cheese.
2. Pulse these ingredients, adding the water slowly until a mealy consistency is formed, about 1-2 minutes.
3. Transfer the dough to a floured work surface and form into a round shape. Using a rolling pin, roll out to a ¼-inch thickness, approximately 12 inches in diameter.
4. Carefully place in 10-inch pie pan, fold edges, and crimp uniformly.

Continued on next page…

Quiche
1 roasted red pepper
2 teaspoons oil
1 bunch spinach
1 onion, thinly sliced
4 large eggs
1¼ cups milk
1 teaspoon salt
¼ teaspoon nutmeg (optional)
1 cup shredded Cheddar/Jack cheese
½ cup feta crumbles

1. Heat the oven to 400° F.
2. Roast the peppers over an open flame until blackened. Allow them to cool, peel the skin off, de-stem and remove the seeds. Slice into thin strips.
3. Heat 1 teaspoon of oil in a large pan, add the spinach and cook until just wilted, remove it from the pan to a cutting board and chop into small pieces. In the pan, sauté the onions over medium heat with 1 teaspoon of oil until they are caramelized (a golden brown) and allow them to cool.
4. In a large mixing bowl, whisk the eggs, milk, salt and nutmeg together.
5. Spread the onions evenly over the crust, then layer the shredded cheese, spinach, red peppers and feta on top. Pour the egg mixture over all this and bake at 400° F for 1 hour. Remove from the oven and let cool for 15 minutes before slicing into wedges.

COSMIC FRIED RICE

Fried rice is a breakfast staple in Hawaii, offered as an alternative to hash browns. Local "Kine" (Hawaiian slang often used for proper names) where I worked would prepare fried rice for the staff meal, throwing in bacon, Portuguese sausage and ham. This version is slightly healthier and one we often use at Cosmic Kitchen to accompany the daily special of grilled fish and mixed green salad.

~ Makes 4 servings ~

1 cup Fajita Veggies (pg. 115)
2 large eggs
1 tablespoon garlic, minced
1 tablespoon ginger, minced
1 tablespoon canola oil
1 tablespoon sesame oil
2 cups cooked short-grain brown or white rice
2 tablespoons soy sauce
1 tablespoon oyster sauce
½ cup sliced green onions
chopped cilantro

1. Chop the Fajita Veggies into a small dice. Beat the eggs in a bowl and mince the garlic and ginger.
2. In a large wok or skillet, heat 1 tablespoon of canola oil over medium heat. Add the sesame oil, garlic, ginger, Fajita Veggies and sauté for 3 minutes, then remove the veggies from the pan.
3. Add the eggs to the pan and scramble them. Throw the veggies back in, along with the rice, and sauté together as you stir in the oyster and soy sauces. Turn off the heat, fold in the green onions and cilantro and serve immediately.

COSMIC REDSKIN POTATOES

People often ask me how an Irish guy ended up cooking great Mexican food. I was born and raised in Dublin, Ireland, where there was no Mexican food at all. I originally came to the U.S. on a student visa, first to Cape Cod then Phoenix, Arizona, (where Michelle and I met). I worked at my first Mexican restaurant as a busboy. Since then, I've worked alongside Mexicans throughout my career from Coronado, California, to Kailua, Hawaii, even Homer, Alaska – all hardworking, good compadres and I picked up a few recipes along the way.

~ Makes enough for 6-8 servings ~

6 large redskin potatoes cut into 1 inch cubes
¼ cup yellow onions, sliced thin
1 teaspoon granulated garlic
1 teaspoon salt
½ teaspoon black pepper
½ cup cilantro, chopped
2 tablespoons canola oil

1. Place potatoes in a large pot, cover with water and cook approximately 25 minutes, until tender.

2. Drain potatoes and place in a large bowl. Toss in remaining ingredients and serve.

FRENCH TOAST

We use a thick cut eggbread at Cosmic Kitchen, but you can use any bread available, just don't soak it too much in the batter as it will stay soggy. Light, golden brown and delicious is the aim of this recipe.

~ Makes 6-8 servings ~

❖❖❖❖❖❖❖❖❖❖❖

8 large eggs
1½ cups milk
½ cup maple syrup
2 teaspoons sugar
2 teaspoons vanilla
1 teaspoon nutmeg
1 teaspoon cinnamon
4 tablespoons butter
½ loaf of day-old sourdough bread,
or whatever crusty bread is available
(cut into thick slices)

1. Beat the eggs lightly in a bowl. Add in milk, syrup and spices and whisk all together.

2. Heat 1 tablespoon butter until sizzling in a large nonstick fry pan or griddle over medium heat. Dip 3 slices of bread lightly in the batter and then place them in the hot pan for approximately 3 minutes a side or until golden and toasty. Remove to a platter while you repeat step 2 with remaining bread. Serve with warm maple syrup, butter and fresh fruit.

BELGIAN WAFFLE

A little planning and effort pays off, as the browned butter makes an especially addictive breakfast or brunch treat – the family will beg for more!

~ Makes 4 servings ~

½ cup melted butter
1 (4-ounce) package active dry yeast
2 cups milk
1 teaspoon salt
1 teaspoon sugar
2 cups flour
¼ teaspoon baking soda
2 large eggs
cooking spray

1. Melt butter in a small pot over medium heat, cooking until it turns lightly brown with a nutty aroma.
2. Dissolve yeast in ½ cup warm water and set aside until foamy (8-10 minutes).
3. In a large bowl, whisk together the yeast mixture with the melted butter, milk, salt, sugar and flour.
4. Cover with plastic wrap and refrigerate overnight or at least 8 hours.
5. Preheat the waffle iron, then whisk baking soda and eggs into the batter. Spray the waffle iron with cooking spray; pour ¾ cup batter into it, let set for 30 seconds, close lid and cook for 4-5 minutes. Serve with warm syrup and butter.

BLUEBERRY SOURDOUGH PANCAKES

Michelle's dad, "Hambone" Wilson, ate breakfast every day at the restaurant when he and Aileen came up from Florida for the summer. Of course, we never let him pay, his usual order being 2 small pancakes and a couple of eggs. He always laughed when we told him his pancakes only cost about 25 cents and he's worth every penny!

We think long and hard before we raise prices on our menu. In the early days, as we began to grow and offer more fresh, local, organic and high quality products, we realized that a more scientific approach needed to be taken to justify costs and sales on any given item. We now use a program that breaks down every ingredient into pounds and ounces, factoring in a percentage loss of weight after cooking, into equations that result in the true cost of what ends up on your plate. It's a time consuming project we undertake regularly, as meat markets are volatile, and crop failures and seasons cause prices to fluctuate, compelling us to react to market prices.

At the end of the day, we crunch all the numbers and realize that prices must go up to pay the bills, the staff and the overhead. Breakfast has the highest markup of costs on the menu to offset the lower markup of more expensive dinner items. The alchemy of blending price increases is where science meets the art of the restaurateur.

So mixing up a batch of these cakes will help your budget and maybe even allow you to splurge on high quality maple syrup, from virgin forests if you please.

~ Makes 12 Pancakes ~

Sourdough Starter

2 cups flour
1 cup flour (for later use)
1 (4-ounce) package active dry yeast
2 tablespoons sugar
2 cups warm water (boiled or filtered)

1. Mix 2 cups of flour, yeast, sugar and water in a glass or ceramic bowl, cover with a towel and store in a warm place.
2. Stir the starter every 12 hours and once daily add in a ¼ cup of flour with a little water (until you have the consistency of pancake batter) for 4-5 days.
3. It's ready to use on the fifth day, after which you can store the starter in the fridge for up to 10 days.
Note: Before using again, bring the starter to room temperature, feed it with flour and water, and let it ferment 8-12 hours more.

Blueberry Pancakes

2½ cups flour
1 teaspoon salt
½ cup sugar
1 teaspoon baking soda
½ teaspoon baking powder
2 cups milk
2 eggs
1 tablespoon vanilla
1 cup sourdough starter
1 tablespoon butter
1 cup blueberries

1.   In a large bowl, whisk together the flour, salt, sugar, baking soda and powder. Add in the milk, eggs, vanilla and sourdough, mix until everything is smooth.
2. Heat a nonstick frying pan over medium high heat. Grease it up with a tablespoon of butter to get started.
3.   Drop in dollops of the pancake mixture, sprinkling 7-8 blueberries over each cake. As they start to bubble, flip them over and cook 3-4 minutes on the other side until golden. Serve with whipped butter and warm maple syrup.

INTERSTELLAR SANDWICHES AND SALADS

TIKKA LEAH
PITA SANDWICH

It takes a village to raise a restaurant and that includes our wonderful staff, who over the years has contributed ideas and specials such as the Tikka Leah . Hopefully we've inspired them to find their own way in the world and that no matter what their career choice, we've encouraged them to have a positive, hard-working outlook, keeping high standards and consistency.

All of our staff are stars and none more so than Leah Tufares who created this sandwich for a special one day. Very often Leah takes your order, cooks your food and serves it to you as well, while it seems the rest of us struggle to keep up. I think someday she could be President (of Cosmic Kitchen!)

~ Makes enough for 2 ~

Tikka Spice Mix
1 tablespoon cumin
1 tablespoon cayenne
1 tablespoon thyme
1 tablespoon granulated garlic
1 tablespoon paprika
2 tablespoons curry powder

Whisk all the spices together in a bowl and store in a container with a tightly fitted lid.

Chicken Tikka
2 tablespoons Tikka Spice Mix
2 (5-ounce) boneless, skinless chicken breasts
2 tablespoons canola oil

1. Measure 2 tablespoons of Tikka Spice onto a platter, roll the chicken breasts in this, and then pour the oil over it.
2. Heat up the grill (or a cast iron skillet) to medium heat and cook the chicken 4 to 5 minutes each side until fully cooked (reading 165° F inside with a meat thermometer). Allow to cool down and slice into thin strips.

Continued on next page…

Tikka Leah
2 pitas
2 tablespoons Tzatziki Sauce (pg. 58)
shredded lettuce
tomato slices
avocado slices
red pepper slices
2 teaspoons Anna's Chutney (pg. 37)

1. Toast the pita on the grill then smear the Tzatziki Sauce over it. Top with lettuce, tomato, avocado, peppers and chicken, then finish off with the chutney and wrap in foil.

Get creative; invent your own pita Tikka, as we always need a new special. – Thanks, Leah!

ANNA'S MANGO CHUTNEY

We use a lot of chutney, mainly on our Chicken Tikka sandwiches and salads. This recipe was given to me by one of our employees who moved to India. I use frozen mangos as this is Alaska! But you can try chutney with any fruit you like, even tomatoes! And canning is a great way to save summer abundance for our long winters.

~ Makes about one Pint ~

⅔ cups sugar
⅔ cups distilled white vinegar
2-inch piece of fresh ginger root, minced
4 garlic cloves
2 pounds very firm mangos, peeled & cut into small pieces
½-1 tablespoon chili powder
1 tablespoon mustard seeds
1 tablespoon salt
⅔ cup raisins or golden raisins
½ teaspoon garam masala

1. Place the sugar and all but 1 tablespoon of vinegar in a saucepan and simmer for 10 minutes.
2. Blend the ginger, garlic, and remaining vinegar to a paste in a blender or food processor. Add to the pan and cook for 10 minutes, stirring.
3. Add the mango and remaining ingredients to the pan and cook, uncovered, for about 25 minutes, stirring as the chutney thickens.
4. Remove from the heat and allow cooling. Pour into hot sterilized jars, making sure that the lids are airtight.

RED LENTIL
QUINOA BURGER

⅓ cup red lentils
½ cup quinoa
2 cups water
6 mushrooms
½ small zucchini
1 sweet potato (baked or microwaved)
5 tablespoons olive oil
2 cloves garlic, minced
¼ teaspoon red pepper flakes
2 teaspoons all purpose seasoning blend
¾ cup bread crumbs
1½ teaspoons lemon juice

Homer is a quirky town with its fair share of "end of the roaders" or refugees from the mainstream; I guess that is why we fit in so well. We have fond memories of our friend, Brother Asaiah, whose '60's-style sect of Barefooters set up a homestead commune at the head of Kachemak Bay. He donated a parcel of land (close to Cosmic Kitchen) on Pioneer Avenue called WKFL Park with a large granite rock in the middle of it. The motto of the Barefooters is on a plaque attached to the monolith, "WKFL — wisdom, knowledge, faith, and love."

Brother Asaiah attended every church in Homer and every restaurant, dishing out kudos to all. His favorite breakfast was Biscuits & "Groovy." We serve a lot of burgers at Cosmic Kitchen — avocado bacon cheeseburgers, salmon, halibut, buffalo burgers, and, of course, WKFL burgers (for our vegetarians and vegans). We believe Brother Asaiah would love this recipe for Red Lentil Quinoa Burgers.

We honor Brother every year by contributing to a special fund he set up with The Homer Foundation, helping our community's children through Homer Head Start.

~ Makes enough for 8 ~

1. Combine the lentils and quinoa with the water in a medium saucepan and bring to a boil. Turn heat down to simmer for about 10 minutes, then turn off heat and allow to cool while you prep the rest of the recipe.
2. Chop the mushrooms into small pea-sized pieces, same with the zucchini. Scoop out the flesh of the sweet potato, discard the skin.

Continued on next page…

3. Heat 1 tablespoon oil over medium heat; add the mushrooms and zucchini and sauté 2 to 3 minutes. Then add the garlic, red pepper flakes and seasoning and cook a couple of minutes longer. Transfer to a large bowl.

4. Mix in the quinoa and lentils, sweet potato, bread crumbs, and lemon juice until thoroughly combined, then refrigerate for 30 minutes or up to four hours.

5. Divide the mixture into 8 patties, pressing firmly together with your hands. Heat 4 tablespoons of oil in a pan over medium heat and fry the patties approximately 2 minutes per side each or until golden brown. Build the burgers with toasted whole wheat buns; add pickles, avocado and tomato slices, if desired.

~ Makes enough for 4 ~

SWEET POTATO FRIES

2 sweet potatoes or yams
½ cup rice flour
1 teaspoon garlic powder
1 teaspoon chili powder
½ teaspoon salt
2 tablespoons lemon juice
2 teaspoons soy sauce
1 cup canola oil

1. Peel and cut the potatoes into finger sized "fries".
2. Mix the flour, spices and salt in a bowl, and the lemon juice and soy sauce in another bowl.
3. Toss the fries first with the lemon/soy mix and then in the flour mix until all well coated.
4. Heat the oil in a large fry pan over medium heat. Fry the potatoes in two batches so as not to overcrowd the pan, about 8 to 10 minutes per batch.

FALAFEL

It's not unusual in Homer for small businesses to close up shop for a couple of weeks so everyone on staff can take a break and go somewhere warm like Mexico or Hawaii. It's also a good time for the "ship" to get an overhaul with equipment repair, painting and cleaning. We've never found a twin of Cosmic Kitchen "Outside" (as Alaskans call the lower states), a restaurant that could command our loyalty serving breakfast, lunch, dinners and Mexican food along with iconic menu items of Gyros, Tikka, Chorizo and Falafel.

It's no wonder you all get so excited when we reopen, after having to cook "so much" and being deprived for "so long". So here it is in case you're craving Falafel; now you've got the recipe, read it carefully and follow through so you don't get withdrawals while we're away.

~ Makes 20 Falafels ~

1¼ pounds dried chickpeas
1 cup water
2 teaspoons baking soda
1 yellow onion, chopped
2 cloves garlic, minced
1 bunch cilantro, chopped
1 bunch Italian parsley, chopped
1 tablespoon cumin
1 tablespoon coriander
1 tablespoon curry powder

1. Soak the chickpeas overnight in a large bowl covered by at least 4 inches of water with 1 teaspoon of the baking soda.
2. Chop the onion, mince the garlic and roughly chop the cilantro and parsley.
3. Drain the chickpeas and puree them in a food processor until finely ground, then transfer to a large bowl.
4. Continue using the food processor with the onion, garlic, cilantro and parsley, puree for about 1 minute then add to the bowl also.
5. Combine the cumin, coriander, curry, red and black pepper and salt into the chickpeas.

Continued on next page…

1½ teaspoons red pepper flakes
1½ teaspoons black pepper
1 tablespoon salt
1 teaspoon baking powder
1 cup chickpea flour

6. Mix the baking powder and the rest of the baking soda into 1 cup of water and add this into the falafel mix along with the chickpea flour. Cover and refrigerate for at least 1 hour.

7. Heat a deep pot with 4 to 5 inches of oil (or a fryer) to 350° F. Using a small ice cream scoop gently roll the falafel balls into the oil in batches so as not to overload it.

8. Drain on paper towels and serve with warm pita, avocado, tomato and Tzatziki Sauce (pg. 58).

BBQ CHICKEN SALAD

This salad is a wonderful addition to your kitchen combining recipes that may be used throughout the week when you need a quick lunch or snack.

~ Makes 4 servings ~

1 pound romaine blend (romaine w/ iceberg, carrots, and red cabbage)
1 cup Ranch Dressing (recipe follows)
½ cup Marinated Cucumber (pg. 58)
1 tomato, diced
1 avocado, sliced thickly
1 cup Sean's Corn Relish (pg. 141)
4 slices bacon, cooked crispy & crumbled
½ cup shredded Cheddar/Jack cheese
4 breasts Aloha Marinated Grilled Chicken
(pg. 103), cut into ½ inch cubes
½ cup BBQ Sauce (recipe follows)
½ bunch cilantro, chopped
1 lime cut in quarters

1. Place the mixed greens in large bowl and toss lightly with the dressing.
2. Divide the salad among 4 large chilled salad bowls. Top each salad with the vegetables, bacon and cheese.
3. Toss the chicken with the BBQ Sauce, divide evenly on the salads, and garnish with cilantro and limes.
Serve immediately.

Continued on next page…

BBQ Sauce
1 cup ketchup
⅔ cup brown sugar
½ cup blackstrap molasses
4 tablespoons yellow mustard
4 tablespoons apple cider vinegar
4 tablespoons vegetable oil
1 tablespoon minced garlic
3 teaspoons chili powder
1 teaspoon ground black pepper
1 teaspoon hot sauce
½ teaspoon ground cloves
½ teaspoon ground allspice
1 teaspoon salt

Ranch Dressing
1 garlic clove
1 cup buttermilk
¼ cup sour cream
½ cup mayonnaise
2 teaspoons oregano
pinch of salt

In a 4-quart saucepan bring all ingredients to a simmer over medium heat, and cook for 20 minutes longer. Remove from heat and let cool. Sauce may be refrigerated for up to a week.

Chop the garlic in a food processor. Add remaining ingredients and blend for 1 minute.

BLACKENED HALIBUT CAESAR SALAD

Homer is considered to be the halibut fishing capital of the world, so an abundance of this mild, white, flaky fish calls for many creative ways to prepare it. Our Blackened Halibut Caesar is served in a taco shell and garnished with avocado for a Mexican touch. We have customers drive down from Soldotna (1½ hours away) just for this salad.

~ Makes 4 servings ~

Blackening Seasoning
½ teaspoon cayenne
2 teaspoons onion powder
2 teaspoons garlic powder
2 teaspoons brown sugar
2 teaspoons salt
½ teaspoon black pepper
½ teaspoon thyme
½ teaspoon oregano
3 tablespoons paprika

Combine all ingredients in a bowl and stir.

Caesar Dressing
5 cloves garlic, minced
1 tablespoon anchovy paste
1 egg (optional)
1 teaspoon Worcestershire sauce
¼ teaspoon black pepper
3 tablespoons red wine vinegar
½ teaspoon Dijon mustard
¼ cup lemon juice
¼ cup parmesan cheese
1½ cups olive oil

Blend all in a food processor until smooth.

Continued on next page…

Salad

3 teaspoons canola oil

1-1½ pounds of halibut filet, remove skin and bones

1 pound romaine blend (romaine w/ iceberg, carrots and red cabbage)

½ cup Caesar Dressing

¼ cup shredded parmesan

4 (10-inch) flour tortillas, deep fried into a bowl shape

1 avocado, peeled, pitted, and cubed

½ cup Marinated Cucumber (pg. 58)

½ cup diced tomatoes

1. Heat a cast iron skillet until very hot; add the canola oil.
2. Dip the halibut in the blackening spice, coat both sides, and then gently slip them into the skillet, frying on both sides approximately 5 minutes each.
3. Toss the greens with the dressing, adding in parmesan cheese and divide among the shells.

Garnish with avocado, cucumbers and tomatoes. Top with slices of the blackened halibut.

COSMIC CHICKEN SALAD

It's all Cosmic, whether it's a burrito, salad, breakfast, or living in Homer – it's Cosmic! Our most popular salad is a mash up of various places and restaurants I have worked in! (Over 40...it was time to open my own!)

~ Makes 4 servings ~

1 pound romaine blend (romaine w/iceberg, carrots and red cabbage)
1 cup Honey Mustard Dressing (recipe follows)
½ cup Marinated Cucumbers (pg. 58)
1 tomato, diced
1 avocado, thinly sliced
½ red pepper, thinly sliced
½ cup shredded Cheddar/Jack cheese
4 Chicken Tikka (pg. 33)
½ cup Anna's Mango Chutney (pg. 37)
1 bunch cilantro, chopped

1. In a large bowl toss the lettuce and honey mustard until lightly coated.
2. Divide lettuce mix among 4 chilled salad plates and add cucumbers, tomatoes, avocados, peppers, cheese and chicken evenly. Top the chicken with chutney and garnish with cilantro.

Honey Mustard Dressing
2 garlic cloves
¼ cup apple cider vinegar
½ cup honey
¼ cup Dijon mustard
½ teaspoon salt
2 cups canola oil

Mince the garlic in a food processor. Add the vinegar, honey, mustard, and blend for 2 minutes. Add the salt and gradually blend in the oil to form a smooth emulsion.

GREEK SALAD

This is another one of our most popular salads (and sandwiches also.) Gyros, pronounced "Year-ohs" is delicious. We grill it till its crispy yet moist and it's a nice balance of Mediterranean style lamb and spices, whether over mixed greens or in a warm pita with Tzatziki Sauce.

Gyros is hard to find so this recipe for lamb meatballs will substitute nicely; even your Greek friends will be impressed.

~ Makes 4 servings ~

1 pound ground lamb
3 cloves garlic, minced
⅓ cup yellow onion
1 teaspoon ground allspice
½ teaspoon ground coriander
1 tablespoon oregano
½ teaspoon salt
½ teaspoon black pepper
2 tablespoons red wine

Combine all ingredients in a bowl and knead together with your hands. Divide into approximately sixteen pieces, rolling into little balls, which you can thread onto bamboo skewers for grilling or pan frying until well browned on all sides but juicy on the inside.

For the salad use a blend of Italian mixed greens, with kalamata olives, tomatoes, cucumbers, red peppers, feta cheese, Tzatziki Sauce (pg. 58) and warm pita. Top with the gyro meatballs hot off the grill.

Marinated Cucumbers

1 cucumber, peeled with a zester and sliced thinly
2 tablespoons rice wine or cider vinegar
2 tablespoons sugar
2 teaspoons dill
salt and pepper to taste

Mix all ingredients in a bowl and toss lightly. Chill in fridge until ready to use.

Tzatziki Sauce

1 cucumber, grated by hand
2 garlic cloves, finely chopped
1 cup plain yogurt
1 tablespoon Italian Parsley, finely chopped
salt and pepper

Grate cucumber and squeeze out excess liquid by hand. Place in a bowl and mix with garlic, yogurt, parsley and season with salt and pepper.

COLESLAW

I was impressed by the variety of salads available while working in Switzerland. They called them "Gemischter salad", mixed compositions such as beet root, celery root, rice, pasta salad, and even sliced meats as salad. A perfect dinner for us at home consists of a Gemischter salad, a cup of soup, and a crusty slice of bread. Coleslaw and potato salad are always nice to have on hand to start composing your own variations. Just arrange it nicely on a plate, give it a fancy name, like 'Misto" or "Gemischter" and let the compliments roll in.

~ Makes 6-8 servings ~

1 large head green cabbage
1 medium carrot
½ cup onion, diced
1½ cups mayonnaise
¼ cup apple cider vinegar
½ cup sugar
1 teaspoon black pepper

1. Shred the cabbage as thin as you can into a large bowl.

2. Peel and julienne the carrot into thin strips, adding this to the bowl, along with the remaining ingredients.

Stir well and allow to set for one hour. It's even better the second day.

MOM'S POTATO SALAD

3 pounds red-skin potatoes (about 8)
½ cup mayonnaise
1½ tablespoons Dijon mustard
¼ cup dill pickle juice from the jar
1 teaspoon sugar
1¼ teaspoons salt
¼ teaspoon black pepper
5 hard-boiled eggs, peeled
2 tablespoons chopped red onion
2 tablespoons Italian parsley, chopped
Paprika for garnish

Our moms had a lot in common when it comes to food: they were both very good cooks, always planning and making dinner for the family, never fancy but frugal, earthy food that we still reminisce about. They considered cooking "a chore," something to get done with as quickly as possible. The idea of blogging, Instagram, or obsessing about food didn't occur to that generation.

They say you can never go home again, but try this potato salad recipe, and at least you can visit for awhile in the land of comfort.

~ Makes 8-10 servings ~

1. Cut the potatoes into quarters and place in a large pot with enough water to cover them by 2 inches. Bring to a boil and simmer for 20-25 minutes, or until tender.

2. Meanwhile, whisk in a small bowl the mayonnaise, Dijon mustard, pickle juice, sugar, salt and pepper.

3. Drain the potatoes into a large bowl and allow to cool slightly.

4. Add the dressing, eggs, onions and parsley to potatoes and stir vigorously with a wooden spoon, mashing up the eggs. Season to taste with more salt and pepper if you like, and garnish with paprika.

SPIT HAPPENS!

One of the most surreal experiences for me was flying in a small commuter plane from Anchorage. The pilot, Gerald (a regular customer), must have unknowingly sensed my excitement by taking a celebratory lap out over the spit whereby, from the air, we could view our second restaurant running smoothly below us. I had achieved success finally at this stage in my life and was flying back to Homer having been sworn in as a U.S. Citizen (another late blooming achievement). It was a thrill to land in the town that had welcomed and encouraged us to become part of its fabric, for which we're forever grateful.

A jumping off point for all activities such as

kayaking, hiking and fishing charters, the Homer

Spit is a magnet for a wide variety of interests. With a lot of shops, restaurants and the world famous Salty Dawg bar for entertainment, it's like the "Key West" of Alaska or aka "A quaint little drinking town with a fishing problem."

We sell our coffee mugs, T-shirts, C.D.s, plants, even the art on the walls, and, of course, bumper stickers like "Keep Homer Weird", "We're here because we're not all there" and "Spit Happens" – does it ever!

Customers always ask us when we are going to open a Cosmic Kitchen in their hometown, from Juneau to Fairbanks, so a few years into our adventure, we settled on a location a little closer, out on the Homer Spit.

The spit is actually a four-mile road out into the middle of Kachemak Bay, attracting tourists and fisherman for the short summer season. Locals like

to brag they never go out there, but secretly we all enjoy its pleasures.

So again, we took the plunge and bought the Silver Fox charter boat office and proceeded to convert it into a restaurant. We built another kitchen from scratch, new exhaust system, bathroom and dining room, all up to code, for the summer season. We hired and trained a second crew who loaded up product from the Cosmic Kitchen in town every morning and headed out to do business on the spit. Like the rest of Alaska, business starts off slowly at the beginning of summer, peaks in July, then winds down again as school starts and fishing slows also.

We learned from the spit that running two restaurants is an all-consuming enterprise. Being busy out there increased the work load of the town location, even taking some key staffers out to help in a pinch. After a few summers, we realized that we had to sacrifice the spit store to concentrate on our young town business; it just wasn't worth our divided attention for such a short summer clientele.

We learned the limits of what we can or want to do and even with one restaurant, still struggle to balance any semblance of personal life with business life. We've come to peace with the fact that the two are interchanged, the small business owner is always on duty. I guess it's true that when we go out, we'll always tacitly observe other operations' service, ambiance, prices, etc..., knowing that's "us" in other businesses' failures and successes, though we like to think we have more of the latter.

A lot of townspeople can wistfully recall the first place on the spit where they camped out upon arriving in town, to work at the cannery or eventually homesteading up in the hills. "Spit rats" lived in tent villages, often just tarps and driftwood, but we had a trailer that we parked close to the "fishing hole." Though we arrived after the cannery heydays (it burnt down), some of it lives on, recycled as Cosmic Kitchen's hot line shelving just in case you have déjà-vu when you come in – Spit Happens!

Michelle and I ride our bicycles out and back regularly on the spit trail, now extended all the way to Land's End, where we both worked together in the early years. Where else in the world can you see glaciers, volcanoes, whales, otters and other fascinating spit life from the same trail? You're also likely to spot another unusual shorebird, the

"kitesurfer," who is an increasingly popular species since I was the first one doing it off the spit in 2000. Like the golden plover, we migrated between Alaska and Hawaii for a few years before finally settling in Homer and I brought the nascent sport of kiting with me. It was so new then that after 911 was called by people thinking a plane had crashed in the bay, the

The spit is perfect for kitesurfing, with its onshore breeze and long sandy beaches, even world

local police suggested I let them know before going out so they could assure worried callers that everything is OK.

famous kitesurfer Robby Naish, from Hawaii, has discovered it (with, of course, post-session "grinds" at Cosmic Kitchen).

Alas! Business calls and some "stoked" days kiting have been forfeited to the onslaught of summer madness. In Alaska, we have to make the most of the busy times, and I can't let customers or the crew down with a "gone kiting" sign, though the thought has crossed my mind.

STARMAN'S GALAXY OF SOUPS

ROASTED RED PEPPER AND SMOKED GOUDA

Michelle and I lived in Zurich, Switzerland for a year while I did a "stagiaire," or chef apprenticeship, in a large hotel chain called Môvenpick. I learned a great deal of European-style cooking organization and use of seasonal menus, that still inspire my ideas at Cosmic Kitchen for specials or "actions" as they call it.

Michelle was ineligible to work in Switzerland and passed her time visiting with all the different staff at the hotel (13 different nationalities) who welcomed us and shared their stories and love of food and wine from their homelands. In Switzerland, fondue parties were regular events, at which we learned the art of dipping Kirschwässer (cherry brandy) laden chunks of bread into the fondue!

Our grand tour of European education ended mercifully after my stagiaire was up—we couldn't take much more partying, but I guess this cheese infused recipe is homage to my time in Switzerland. Feel free to dip a chunk of crusty bread into the soup with or without kirsch!

~ Makes 2 Quarts ~

4 red peppers
1 tablespoon canola oil
½ cup onion, diced
1 tablespoon tomato paste
½ teaspoon white pepper
1 tablespoon paprika
1 tablespoon granulated garlic
6 cups chicken or vegetable broth
2 pounds smoked Gouda, shredded
½ cup flour

Garnish: ⅓ cup green onions or chives, sliced

1. Roast the red peppers over an open flame or grill till blackened. Peel, remove seeds and cut into large chunks.
2. In a large soup pot, heat the oil over medium heat. Add peppers, onions, paste, spices and sauté for 3-5 minutes.
3. Add the broth, bring to a boil and simmer for 20 minutes.
4. Mix shredded cheese and flour in a large bowl.
5. Turn off the heat. Use blender to puree the soup, gradually adding in the cheese/flour mixture. Bring soup back to a simmer for another 10 minutes. Don't forget the crusty bread and to garnish with green onions or chives.

SWEET POTATO CORN CHOWDER

In Honolulu I worked for Marriott Corporation at the University of Hawaii. It was a great introduction to high volume catering, Hawaiian style cuisine and also the Shintani diet, which was a new concept to promote healthy eating. I helped develop the menus that we offered to students to encourage the use of natural and local products such as fish, sweet potatoes, corn and fruit which Hawaii is known for but had been lost in the progress of busy lives and modern convenience.

This recipe utilized Kahuku corn, Okinawa sweet potatoes and soy milk to entice students away from pizza and fries. I still think of Kahala, Lanikai, and Manoa when I make this soup and look forward to our local farmer's market veggies and greens to brighten our summer fare.

~ Makes 4 servings ~

½ yellow onion
2 ribs celery
½ red pepper
1 carrot
3 sweet potatoes (or yams)
¼ cup butter
2 teaspoons thyme
1 teaspoon granulated garlic
2 bay leaves
½ cup flour
4 cups vegetable broth
1 (12-ounce) bag frozen corn
½ cup heavy cream or soy milk
½ teaspoon white pepper

1. First, prep the veggies: chop the onions, celery, peppers and carrots into pea-sized pieces. Peel and cut the potatoes into ½-inch cubes.
2. Melt the butter in a large soup pot over medium heat. Add in all veggies, thyme, granulated garlic, bay leaves and sauté for a couple of minutes.
3. Add in the sweet potatoes and flour, stirring well until everything is coated and sticky.
4. Pour in the veggie broth slowly and bring to a boil. Add in the corn and simmer for 20 minutes.
5. Turn off the heat, add in the heavy cream (or soy milk) and season with white pepper.

MEXICAN CHICKEN TORTILLA SOUP

This is another much requested soup and recipe at Cosmic Kitchen. Basically, it's a variation of our Enchilada sauce with veggies and beans thrown in, garnished with tortilla chips. Make it and people will think you're a culinary genius – we take credit where we can get it!

~ Makes 4 servings ~

2 whole dried Ancho chiles
½ yellow onion
1 carrot
½ red pepper
1 tablespoon canola oil
1 tablespoon ground cumin
1 tablespoon granulated garlic
1 tablespoon chili powder
1 tablespoon dried oregano
1 bay leaf
1 teaspoon salt
½ teaspoon black pepper
1 (14.5-ounce) can diced tomatoes
¼ cup tomato paste
4 cups vegetable broth
2 cups cooked chicken, diced or shredded
1 (15-ounce) can red kidney beans
½ cup frozen corn kernels
1 tablespoon lime juice
4 corn tortillas (cut into 1-inch squares)

1. Place the Ancho chiles in a bowl and cover with hot water to soak until softened, at least 20 minutes.
2. Chop the onion, carrot and pepper into small ½ inch pieces.
3. Heat the oil in a large soup pot over medium heat; add the veggies and sauté 3-4 minutes. Then add the dried spices, salt and pepper, tomatoes and paste, stirring all the time so the paste doesn't stick to the bottom.
4. Add in the veggie broth, bring to a boil, and let simmer for 20 minutes.
5. Drain the chiles, remove the stems and puree in a food processor. Add this paste into the simmering veggies.
6. Add in the chicken, kidney beans and corn kernels, stirring well.
7. Pulse the corn tortillas in the food processor for 30 seconds, then add to soup, along with the lime juice.

Garnish with avocado, cilantro and tortilla chips.

TOMATO BASIL BISQUE

I have a few goals in mind with this cookbook – first is to offer it as a souvenir for our summer clientele or as a "How to" manual for college kids leaving town for their first year away. Another goal is an answer to the requests for recipes we get. But, surprisingly, most of all I'm looking forward to having the cookbook as a guideline to our staff who produce the food daily using word of mouth and repetition for their recipes. At last I can say "it's on page 56 – trust me it works!"

~ Makes 4 servings ~

¼ cup olive oil
1 onion, diced
1 teaspoon garlic, minced
1 teaspoon oregano
1 teaspoon basil
½ teaspoon thyme
1 bay leaf
2 (14.5-ounce) cans whole tomatoes (preferably San Marzano)
6 ounces tomato paste
1 tablespoon red wine vinegar
1 tablespoon honey or sugar
1 teaspoon salt
¼ teaspoon pepper
2 quarts vegetable broth
1 cup heavy cream

1. Heat the oil in a large soup pot over medium heat. Add the onions and sauté for 2-3 minutes.

2. Add garlic, herbs, tomatoes, paste, vinegar, sugar, and salt and pepper, stirring continuously.

3. Add the vegetable broth, bring to a boil and simmer for 20 minutes.

4. Turn off heat and puree with an immersion blender, return to a low simmer and add in the heavy cream. For more refined tomato bisque, use a food-mill instead of a blender.

HUNGARIAN MUSHROOM SOUP

This is by far our most popular soup. A rich umami mushroom flavor with a hint of dill, paprika and finished with sour cream causes our customers to plan their next visit to Cosmic Kitchen based on its availability. Usually we post our daily specials, soups and juices on Facebook mid-morning so customers can call in and order their lunch ahead of time. Our busy clientele likes to have their order ready when they arrive, often ordering something extra for later or for a friend back at the office. This soup sells out early so now you can make your own in case you missed it.

~ Makes enough for 6-8 servings ~

¼ pound butter
½ cup onions, diced
1½ pounds mushrooms, sliced
1 tablespoon dill
2 tablespoons paprika
2 tablespoons tomato paste
½ cup flour
6 cups chicken or vegetable stock
½ cup sour cream

1. Melt the butter in a large soup pot. Add the onions and mushrooms, stirring continuously, then add the spices and tomato paste.
2. Add the flour gradually, stirring until the mixture is coated and sticky.
3. Add the broth, bring to a boil and simmer for 20 minutes. Turn off the heat and whisk in the sour cream.

Serve with a nice crusty garlic bread.

SPINACH CLAM CHOWDER

"Did I mention the Bisque?" We don't use much fancy terminology in Homer, the town's motto being "The City That Works" could also be the "City That Prefers Chowder to Bisque!"

Michelle's dad always claimed that he got the "duty" clam, that is, the only one in his bowl as we must have shorted him on clams! So make sure you have enough clams and feel free to throw any other seafood into your chowder so it's hearty enough for all the hardworking critics in your family!

~ Makes 1½ Quarts ~

4 cups fresh spinach
¼ cup butter
½ onion, diced
½ cup flour
1 quart clam juice
½ teaspoon nutmeg
½ teaspoon white pepper
8 ounces frozen chopped clams
½ cup heavy cream

1. First, cook the spinach by heating 2 tablespoons of butter in a large soup pot over medium heat. Add in the spinach and cook until wilted (3-4 minutes). Turn off the heat and pour the spinach into a bowl to cool down.
2. Continue with the same pot, heating the remaining butter over medium heat adding in the diced onions. Stir for 2-3 minutes, then add in the flour to form a paste.
3. Gradually add the clam juice in stages, bring to a boil and simmer for about 10 minutes.
4. Chop up the spinach so there are no long stems or leaves. Add it into the pot along with the nutmeg, pepper and the clams.
5. Simmer for 10 minutes more then turn off the heat and stir in the heavy cream.

Serve with crackers or crusty sourdough bread.

BORSCHT

We rely on winter vegetables a lot here in Homer, Alaska. This soup delights our customers with its vibrant color and taste. Locally grown beets are delicious, delivered by farmers in the nearby Russian village of Nikolaevsk, who also provide us with Yukon gold potatoes, carrots, cucumbers, berries and other produce in season. The trendy farm-to-fork movement has always been a way of life up here, though not necessarily a matter of life and death as an Alaska reality TV show would like you to believe. The characters (and film crew) all dine regularly at the Cosmic Kitchen after shooting their episodes. I wish they would mention us at least once as part of their survival strategy. We know they love our Big Bang Burritos!

~ Makes 1½ Quarts ~

3 beets, peeled and cubed
2 Yukon Gold potatoes
1 yellow onion
1 carrot
2 celery ribs
2 garlic cloves, minced
2 tablespoons canola oil
3 cups vegetable broth
1 teaspoon dried dill
2 tablespoons honey
½ cup rice wine vinegar

Garnish: sour cream

1. Prep the vegetables, peeling and cubing the beets, potatoes, onion and carrot into uniform ½-inch cubes. Dice the celery and mince the garlic.
2. Heat a large soup pot with the oil over medium heat. Toss in the onions and garlic first, then the rest of the veggies and stir-fry for 3-4 minutes.
3. Add in the broth, bring to a boil and simmer for about 40 minutes.
4. Add in the dill, honey, vinegar and cook about 20 minutes longer.

Serve with a dollop of sour cream atop each bowl.

AFRICAN PEANUT STEW

This recipe combines some of my favorite ingredients – curry, ginger, sweet potatoes and peanut butter. Most of these you may already have in your pantry so it's an easy and delicious idea for dinner.

~ Makes enough for 6-8 servings ~

2 celery ribs
1 carrot
1 onion
3 sweet potatoes, peeled
2 tablespoons olive oil
3 garlic cloves, minced
1½ tablespoons fresh ginger, minced
2 teaspoons curry powder
1 teaspoon red chili flakes
2 cups vegetable broth
½ cup diced tomatoes
1 cup peanut butter
2 tablespoons tomato paste
½ teaspoon salt

Garnish: cilantro and green onions

1. Prep the veggies: chop the celery, peel and dice the carrot and onions into ½ inch cubes. Same with the sweet potatoes.
2. In a large soup pot, heat the oil over medium heat. Add the celery, carrot and onion, and sauté for 3-5 minutes. Add the garlic, ginger and potato and cook for another 3 minutes.
3. Add in the curry, chili flakes and veggie broth and bring it to a boil and simmer for 20 minutes.
4. Add in the diced tomatoes, peanut butter, tomato paste, salt and simmer a few minutes longer, stirring well.

Serve with steamed rice and garnish with cilantro and chopped green onions.

THAI CURRY CHICKEN SOUP

This is probably our second most popular soup. Our cold Alaska days (even in summer) are helped along with this warm, exotic curry of lemongrass, coconut milk and ginger. Kaffir lime leaf and lemongrass freeze well, so stock up when you find them and <u>to my staff</u>, "Keep calm and carry on" if you can't.

~ Makes 4 servings ~

2 ribs celery
1 carrot
1 yellow onion
4 cups vegetable broth
1 tablespoon canola oil
2 garlic cloves, minced
2 tablespoons fresh ginger, minced
2 tablespoons red curry paste
3 Kaffir lime leaves
2 stalks lemongrass
2 cups Aloha Marinated Grilled Chicken, diced (pg. 103)
1 (14-ounce) can coconut milk
1 tablespoon cornstarch or arrowroot powder
2 tablespoons brown sugar
¼ cup lime juice

Garnish: fresh basil and sliced green onions

1. Prep the veggies: chop the celery, peel the carrot and slice into half moons, peel and slice the onion thinly.
2. Measure ¼ cup of broth into a glass and set aside.
3. Heat the oil in a large soup pot over medium heat. Add in the veggies and sauté for 3 minutes.
4. Add in the garlic, ginger and curry paste and cook a few more minutes. Then add the Kaffir lime leaf, lemongrass, broth and bring to a boil and simmer for 20 minutes.
5. Add in the cooked chicken and the coconut milk, continue stirring.
6. Mix together the cornstarch with the saved broth (in the glass) until smooth, pour this into the simmering soup and stir until nice and thick, about 1 minute.
7. Turn off heat and whisk in the sugar and lime juice.

Serve with steamed rice, fresh basil and sliced green onions.

POTATO, LEEK & FENNEL SOUP

This recipe is updated with the additions of the licorice flavor of fennel and tarragon that people find intriguing and delicious. We use vegetable broth in most of our recipes so it's easy to please the vegetarians, the vegans, the Las Vegans and the rest of us just trying to eat a little healthier. Keep it Cosmic!

~ Makes 2 Quarts ~

3 russet (baking) potatoes
1 yellow onion
3 medium leeks
1 fennel bulb
1 tablespoon canola oil
3 garlic cloves, minced
1 tablespoon tarragon, dried
4 cups vegetable broth
½ cup heavy cream
salt and white pepper to taste

1. Peel and chop the potatoes into 1 inch cubes. Same with the onion. Cut off the root and tip of the leeks and discard. Slice leeks lengthwise and then crosswise into ½ inch pieces and wash thoroughly in a strainer.
2. Cut the rough outer leaves off the fennel, cut in half, remove the core then chop up in ½ inch pieces.
3. Heat the oil in a stock pot over medium heat. Add the onion and leeks and sauté 3 to 4 minutes. Add the garlic, fennel, tarragon and potatoes and continue to stir.
4. Pour in the vegetable broth, bring to a boil and then simmer for 15 minutes.
5. Turn off heat and puree with an immersion blender (or not if you prefer it chunky – I like it in between) then finish off by whisking in the heavy cream and salt and white pepper to taste.

"BROKE DA MOUTH" CHILI

1 yellow onion
1 red pepper
1 green pepper
1 jalapeño
1½ pounds ground beef
2 cloves garlic, minced
1 tablespoon chili powder
1 teaspoon red chili flakes
1 teaspoon cumin
1 bay leaf
2 cups IPA beer
2 cups vegetable broth
¼ cup tomato paste
1 cup crushed tomatoes
1 (12-ounce) can kidney beans
1 tablespoon Worcestershire sauce
1 tablespoon hot sauce
2 tablespoons brown sugar
1 teaspoon liquid smoke
Garnish: shredded cheddar cheese
and sliced green onions

We hadn't made chili in a while, as we usually offer a vegetarian soup, but one day we decided to make it, and noticed how quickly word of mouth spread. Customers went back to work and, before you know it, others called in looking for bowls of chili to go. So now this recipe is a regular on the rotating schedule of soups. In local Hawaiian slang for something delicious, you might say, "broke da mouth", as in, that's how good it is!

~ Makes "Choke" Chili (a lot!) ~

1. Prep the veggies: chop the onions, peppers and jalapeño into pea sized pieces.
2. Heat a large soup pot over medium heat, add the ground beef and cook it until well done, stirring to break up any lumps.
3. Add in the chopped veggies, garlic and dry spices, stirring to avoid any sticking on the bottom.
4. Add the beer, broth, tomato paste and crushed tomatoes, stirring well.
5. Add in the remaining ingredients, bring to a boil and simmer for 40 minutes.
Garnish with shredded cheese and sliced green onions.

Gumbo Z'Herbes

A meatless gumbo that is supposed to bring friendship and luck.

¼ cup (½ stick) butter
¼ cup all-purpose flour
1 large onion, chopped
1 medium green bell pepper, seeded and chopped
2 stalks celery, chopped
8 green onions, thinly sliced
4 garlic cloves, minced
10 cups water or vegetable stock
3 pounds fresh (or 2 10-ounce frozen packages) collard, turnip or mustard greens
1½ pounds (or 1 10-ounce frozen package) spinach leaves
4 cups shredded green cabbage

2 bay leaves
1 teaspoon dried basil
1 teaspoon dried thyme
¼ teaspoon allspice
¼ teaspoon grated nutmeg
⅛ teaspoon ground cloves
1 tablespoon sugar
½ cup minced fresh parsley
1½ dozen shucked oysters, with their liquid (optional)
2 tablespoons filé powder
½ teaspoon hot-pepper sauce
salt & pepper
4 cups hot cooked white rice

1. In a large heavy saucepan, melt the butter over medium heat. Sprinkle the flour over the butter and cook over medium to medium-high heat, stirring constantly for 6 to 10 minutes, or until the mixture (roux) turns a medium-dark reddish brown. Be careful not to burn it. Add the onion, bell pepper, celery, green onions and garlic, stirring frequently, for 5 minutes, or until the vegetables begin to soften . Stir in the water, greens, spinach, cabbage, bay leaves, thyme, allspice, nutmeg, cloves and sugar. Bring to a boil over medium-high heat. Reduce to low and cook, partially covered, for 30 minutes.
2. Add the parsley and the oysters, with their liquid if desired. Cook uncovered for 5 minutes, or until the

Continued on next page…

edges of the oysters begin to curl. Remove the pan from the heat and stir in the filé powder. Season to taste with hot-pepper sauce, salt and black pepper.

3. To serve, spoon about ½ cup of the hot rice into the bottom of each soup bowl and ladle the gumbo on top.

Serves 8.

My other great passion is for music. I'm fascinated by the process of musical composition and people whose whole life is consumed by their art. We play a lot of world music at Cosmic Kitchen and are retailers of Putumayo Music™ label (www.putumayo.com) — my favorite categories are the groove series, lounge music and Arabic series. It's been said that people who excel at their craft have all spent over 10,000 hours at it before achieving success.

The recipes in this book are also "riffs" from jamming with other chefs, pumping out the food in a groove that not always follows the playbook. Putumayo generously allowed us to share this recipe for Gumbo Z'Herbes but of course you don't have to follow it religiously; be creative, innovative, follow your passion and let your culinary freak flag fly, for a large pot of Gumbo will bring you friendship and luck!

CLOSE ENCOUNTERS OF THE MEXICAN "KINE"

PINTO BEANS

There's always a pot of beans cooking away in our kitchen (sometimes 2 or 3 pots). Along with the soups, sauces and breakfast orders our stove is a very busy place, so we usually schedule a day ahead the order of prep work to accommodate all that needs to be done. This is why soaking the beans overnight is a good idea to save time and space.

~ Makes enough for 10 ~

2 cups dried pinto beans
6 cups water
1 tablespoon salt
1 tablespoon granulated garlic
½ yellow onion, diced
2 tablespoons canola oil

1. Rinse the beans thoroughly, cover with a couple inches of water, and soak for 6 hours or overnight in a large bowl.
2. Drain the beans and place them in a large soup pot; add 6 cups water, bring to a boil, then simmer as you add in the salt, garlic and onion.
3. Cook for 1 to 1½ hours or until soft. Turn off heat and stir in the oil.

Puree with an immersion blender if you like them refried style; we like our pintos whole-bean style.

BLACK BEANS

I'm amazed at the amount of black beans we go through – in burritos, bowls and on combo plates. They are an inexpensive way to feed your family, freeze well and can be delicious soup with the addition of some veggies, chiles and leftover meats. Start with this recipe then get creative.

~ Makes enough for 10 ~

2 cups dried black beans
6 cups water
1 tablespoon salt
1 tablespoon granulated garlic
1 tablespoon cumin
½ yellow onion, diced
2 bay leaves

1. Rinse the beans thoroughly, cover with a couple inches of water, and soak for 6 hours or overnight in a large bowl.

2. Drain the beans and place them in a large soup pot; add 6 cups water, bring to a boil, then simmer as you add in the salt, garlic, cumin, onion and bay leaf.

3. Cook for 1 to 1½ hours or until soft.

ALOHA MARINATED GRILLED CHICKEN

The influence of working in Honolulu, Hawaii, for many years is seen throughout our menu. Pineapple salsa, wasabi halibut, coconut salmon and macadamia nut cookies are some of our Asian inspired recipes. I still wear an Aloha shirt on Fridays and stuff my suitcase with Hawaiian goodies such as guava, lilikoi and kochuchang paste whenever we visit the islands. This pineapple marinade tenderizes and adds flavor to grilled meats such as chicken or steak, so enjoy with Aloha!

½ cup lime juice
¼ cup canola oil
1½ cup pineapple juice
1 teaspoon oregano
¼ cup salt
¼ cup granulated garlic
4 cups water
2 pounds boneless, skinless chicken breast (or steak)

1. Mix all the marinade ingredients together in a large bowl, add the meats into the marinade and refrigerate for at least 6 hours or preferably overnight.
2. Heat up the grill or grill pan to medium-high and lightly grease it with a thin layer of oil.
3. Grill the meat 5 to 6 minutes each side or until a meat thermometer shows an internal temperature of 165° F.

Allow the meat to cool so you can slice or dice it up for use in salads, quesadillas and sandwiches.

SPANISH RICE

We make Spanish rice 2 or 3 times a day — so often that all the kitchen staff knows this recipe by heart, finishing each other's steps like a kitchen ballet so the next batch of rice is ready as the lunch rush peaks to a crescendo.

Take your time at home, whisk it up well, scrape the bottom so the paste doesn't burn, and allow the rice to rest a few minutes longer in order to absorb all the broth.

~ Makes enough for 8 ~

½ yellow onion, diced
2 cups long grain rice
2 tablespoons tomato paste
4 cups vegetable broth
1 teaspoon granulated garlic
½ cup frozen mixed vegetables
1 tablespoon canola oil

1. Heat the oil in a large pot over medium heat.
2. Add the onions and rice, stirring until the rice is lightly toasted.
3. Add in the tomato paste, veggie broth and garlic, stirring well. Bring to a boil, cover and simmer for 10-15 minutes longer.
4. Turn off heat, stir in the frozen mixed veggies, cover and allow all the water to be absorbed, 5-10 minutes longer.

Fluff up rice with a spoon and serve.

ENCHILADA SAUCE

We make gallons of this sauce every day to use with huevos rancheros, smothering burritos, enchiladas and chimichangas. This recipe has a nice balance of heat from the chiles and smooth tomato richness that seems to come from the heart of Mexican cuisine.

~ Makes 2 Quarts ~

6 whole dried Ancho chiles
2 quarts vegetable broth
1 bay leaf
1 tablespoon granulated garlic
½ tablespoon black pepper
½ tablespoon cumin
1 tablespoon chili powder
1 teaspoon salt
1 tablespoon tomato paste
½ cup flour
¼ cup canola oil

1. Soak the chiles in warm water for at least 20 minutes.
2. Place the broth in a large soup pot and bring to a boil as you add in the seasonings and tomato paste.
3. Drain the chiles, saving some of the water. Puree them in a food processor, adding a little water to form a smooth paste, and then add this to the large pot.
4. Simmer the sauce as you make the roux – combining the flour and oil in a small pot over medium heat for a few minutes.
5. Whisk the roux into the large pot and simmer for 10 to 15 minutes more. The sauce should be nice and thick enough to coat the back of a spoon.

Let it cool at least a couple of minutes before using.

FAJITA FISH TACOS

Everybody loves our fish tacos — they're the perfect lunch of seared fresh local halibut with fajita veggies on soft corn tortillas spiced up with a visit to our Cosmic salsa bar. Homer folks also like rockfish and salmon when the season is right, so try it with whatever your local catch is.

~ Makes enough for 4 ~

½ pound halibut filet
1 tablespoon lime juice
1 tablespoon dried oregano
1 teaspoon granulated garlic
5 tablespoons canola oil
½ teaspoon salt
¼ teaspoon black pepper
2 cups Fajita Veggies (pg. 115)
16 (6-inch) corn tortillas (warmed in the oven)

Garnish: guacamole, sour cream, fresh salsa

1. Cut the fish into ½ inch cubes and toss in a bowl with the lime juice, oregano, garlic, 1 tablespoon of oil, and salt and pepper. Cover and marinate for 1 hour or overnight in the fridge.
2. Heat a skillet or griddle to medium hot with 2 tablespoons of oil and sauté the fish 4 to 5 minutes, to a light golden brown. Remove to a platter.
3. Continuing with the hot pan, add 2 tablespoons of oil and sauté the Fajita Veggies for 3 to 4 minutes. Add the fish back into the pan, stirring everything together and turn off the heat.
4. Scoop about ⅓ cup of fajita fish onto each double stacked taco (2 tortillas together are better, as 1 single shell will fall apart).

Serve with guacamole, sour cream and fresh salsa.

*Hint: Cosmic secret – add a teaspoon of Sambal Olek into the sour cream for a spicier punch.

HOMER BURRITO

We offer a lot of vegetarian food at Cosmic Kitchen. I guess our customers have known for a long time that a plant-based diet is healthier for them and the planet. Falafel, veggie burgers, soy sausage and tofu are some of the options available.

You don't have to be a vegetarian to enjoy a Homer burrito, as I'm sure our friend Brother Asaiah would have. He often referred to Homer as the "Cosmic Hamlet by the Sea" in his letters to the local newspaper. So we thought the Cosmic Hamlet ought to have a Cosmic Kitchen and a burrito named in its honor — "The Homer Burrito."

~ Makes enough for 6 ~

3 cups Black Beans (pg. 101)
3 cups Enchilada Sauce (pg. 107)
1½ cups Salsa Fresca (pg. 138)
3 cups Spanish Rice (pg. 105)
1½ cups Guacamole (pg. 143)
1½ cups diced tomato
6 (10-inch) flour tortillas
iceberg lettuce, shredded
1½ cups shredded Cheddar/Jack cheese

1. Cook the beans and enchilada sauce the day before as they can easily be reheated. Prep the Salsa Fresca beforehand, as well.
2. Prepare the rice, guacamole and dice the tomatoes, reheat the beans and sauce.
3. To make the burrito, warm the tortillas, one at a time on a hot pan or griddle and stack them on a plate. Fill the tortilla with a ½ cup each of rice, black beans and top with a handful of lettuce and ¼ cup each of guacamole, salsa and tomatoes. Fold the left and right sides of the tortilla inwards then roll the burrito over so the seam is on the bottom.
4. Top with ½ cup of enchilada sauce and cheese and melt in the oven (or microwave for minute or two).

Serve with tortilla chips and more salsa.

COSMIC CHICKEN BURRITO

Cosmic Kitchen is home to a wide demographic of people: at breakfast we see retirees, at lunch it's the work crowd, and afternoons it's the school crowd of kids, parents and teachers.

We love them all, but it's the kids that steal the show with their Christmas play costumes for the Nutcracker, proud new-moms with Cosmic babies (they eat here so often we claim them as "ours") and, of course, slightly older kids who know their favorite restaurant but can't quite say it yet "where do you want to go for dinner?... Cosmic Chicken!" they say.

So here's the burrito recipe for all you Cosmic Chicken lovers!

~ Makes enough for 6 ~

6 cups Spanish Rice (pg. 105)
3 cups Aloha Marinated Grilled Chicken (pg. 103)
3 cups Enchilada Sauce (pg. 107)
6 tablespoons Guacamole (pg. 143)
2 cups Salsa Fresca (pg. 138)
6 (10-inch) flour tortillas
2 cups shredded Cheddar/Jack cheese

1. Prepare the rice, grill the chicken and cook the enchilada sauce – just follow the recipes! Same with the guacamole and salsa fresca.
2. For the burritos: Warm the tortillas, one at a time, in a hot pan or griddle and stack them on a plate. Fill the tortillas with a cup of rice, ½ cup of chicken, a tablespoon each of guacamole, salsa and cheese. Fold the left and right sides of the tortilla inwards, and then roll the burrito over so the seam is on the bottom.
3. Top with ½ cup of enchilada sauce and cheese and melt in the oven (or microwave for a minute or two).

Serve with tortilla chips and more salsa.

FAJITA VEGGIES

Once you've made your own Fajitas you'll never settle for plain old veggies again. Tossed with lime juice, salt and spices, their rawness is mellowed out and their flavor enhanced by searing in a hot skillet to produce menu favorites such as Fajita fish, Philly Cheesesteak or topped on a Cosmic salad bowl.

~ Makes enough for 6-8 ~

1 green pepper
1 red pepper
1 large tomato
1 yellow onion
1 teaspoon salt
1 teaspoon oregano
1 teaspoon granulated garlic
2 ounces canola oil
1 ounce lime juice

1. Rinse the peppers and tomato, cut them in half. Core and de-seed the peppers and slice them into ¼-inch slices. Cut the tomato into thin wedges. Peel the onion, cut in half and slice thinly.
2. Mix all the veggies in a large bowl, sprinkle the salt, oregano and garlic evenly over them, then the oil and lime juice, mixing everything together. Cover and marinate at least one hour before use or preferably overnight.

Sear in a hot skillet with fresh fish or with grilled chicken or steak for a quick week-night dinner.

CHICKEN ENCHILADAS IN CHOCOLATE MOLE SAUCE

Our specials are a blend of ideas from the weekly staff meetings, aimed to give our regular customers something different from the menu. The special is a creative use of ingredients we already have, such as this recipe for chicken enchiladas with mole sauce. The specials are posted on the menu board as you enter Cosmic Kitchen, along with the daily soup and juice of the day. You can also check out the special on our Facebook page.

~ Makes enough for 4 ~

2 dried Ancho chiles
4 cups vegetable broth
1 tablespoon chili powder
⅓ cup tomato paste
1 tablespoon granulated garlic
2 teaspoons cumin
1 teaspoon nutmeg
5 ounces bittersweet chocolate
3 tablespoons canola oil
4 tablespoons flour
8 (6-inch) corn tortillas
2 cups Aloha Marinated Grilled
Chicken (pg. 103), cubed
2 cups shredded Cheddar/Jack
cheese

Garnish: sour cream, tortilla chips

1. First, soak the Ancho chiles in warm water for at least 20 minutes, then puree in a food processor with a little of the water to form a paste.
2. In a large soup pot, bring the vegetable broth to a boil while adding the Ancho chile paste, chili powder, tomato paste, garlic, cumin, nutmeg and chocolate, simmer for 15 minutes.
3. Heat the oil in a small pot and stir in the flour, cooking the roux for 3 to 4 minutes. Gradually whisk the roux into the large pot and simmer a little longer, then turn off the heat.
4. Warm the tortillas in a hot skillet until soft and pliable, stack them on a plate. Put 2 tortillas on another plate and fill each with ¼ cup of chicken. Roll them up seam-side down, cover with ½ cup of sauce and top with ½ cup of shredded cheese. Place in a hot oven while you make the other enchiladas. Then bake for 5 to 6 minutes until cheese is melted and sauce bubbly around edges.

Serve with sour cream and tortilla chips.

COSMIC NACHOS

Some days it seems everyone wants nachos — steak, chicken, veggies, ground beef and "Cosmic" nachos are the choices at Cosmic Kitchen. Every day we fry up a fresh batch of thin corn tortilla chips, tostadas and taco shells for salads and crispy hard tacos. There is never a dull moment in our kitchen – need a job anyone?

"There is no difference between the music you listen to and the food you eat."
Chef Marcus Samuelsson

~ Makes enough for 2 ~

½ cup Fajita Veggies (pg. 115)
½ cup Aloha Marinated Grilled Chicken, cubed (pg. 103)
½ cup grilled steak, cubed
5 ounces corn tortilla chips (store bought is ok)
½ cup Black Beans (pg. 101)
1½ cups shredded Cheddar/Jack cheese

Garnish: guacamole, sour cream

1. Preheat oven to 375° F. In a hot pan, sauté the Fajita Veggies together with the chicken and steak.

2. Mound the chips onto a heat-proof platter. Top with alternating layers of beans, cheese and sautéed fajita mix. Bake in the oven for 10 to 15 minutes until the cheese is melted and bubbling.

Garnish with guacamole, sour cream and lots of salsa.

MAUI-WOWEE GROUND BEEF

5 pounds of ground beef
1 tablespoon salt
1 teaspoon granulated garlic
½ teaspoon black pepper
1 teaspoon cumin
2 tablespoons chili powder
1 teaspoon dried oregano
1 cup pineapple juice
1 cup water
½ cup tomato paste
1 cup crushed tomatoes

I worked for a company in Hawaii that catered events all over the island. From a fashion show on the 40th floor of a downtown skyscraper to weddings on the north shore and cultural events in Pearl Harbor, it was a fun experience.

It wasn't unusual for the crew to smoke a little Maui-wowee on the way to events, but once they found out that I prefer to remain sober at work, I found myself designated driver of a commercial truck full of catered food, props and a "high" crew offering directions around the island. One time, due to the summer heat or too many u-turns, the top layer of the wedding cake slid off, so a quick pit stop was needed to "right" the cake and cover the damage with leis.

So even though I call this recipe Maui-wowee ground beef, you can rest assured knowing that we're all quite sober at Cosmic Kitchen, despite appearances. Mahalo!

~ Makes enough for 10-12 servings ~

1. Cook the ground beef in a large pot over medium heat, stirring regularly until well done. Drain off excess fat leaving 2 tablespoons of it for flavor.
2. Add in all the remaining ingredients, stirring well to avoid scorching on the bottom as it simmers for 15 to 20 minutes.

Turn off heat and scoop it onto nachos, into tacos and burritos. I even use it in Moussaka (pg. 153).

BBQ CHICKEN AND BACON QUESADILLA

Quesadillas are flour tortillas filled with cheese and savory ingredients, folded over and grilled until golden brown. Nowadays, we often get asked for gluten free versions using corn tortillas. We also offer lettuce wraps for people who don't want a bun, brown rice for white, wheat tortillas, tofu and a myriad other dietary requests, all of which we're happy to accommodate.

This recipe uses BBQ chicken, bacon and corn salsa but you can substitute any leftovers from your fridge, or as we call it in the restaurant business, "Today's Special".

~ Makes 4 Quesadillas ~

2 cups Aloha Marinated Grilled Chicken, cubed (pg. 103)
4 tablespoons BBQ Sauce (pg. 48)
4 (10-inch) flour tortillas
4 cups shredded Cheddar/Jack cheese
4 strips crispy bacon, crumbled
4 tablespoons Sean's Corn Relish
(pg. 141)
Garnish: guacamole, sour cream

1. Preheat a skillet or griddle over medium heat and lightly grease it up with a non-stick spray.
2. Toss the chicken in a bowl with the BBQ Sauce.
3. Place one tortilla in the pan and sprinkle ¼ each of the cheese, chicken, bacon and corn relish evenly over it. Fold in half, flip it over and grill until golden and crispy.
4. Repeat with the other tortillas.

Cut each into 4 wedges and serve with guacamole and sour cream.

COSMIC FAMILY

Though colorful from the start, Cosmic Kitchen has blossomed over the years from contributions and collaborations with various artists, craftsmen, and tradesmen.

Thanks to artists such as Carla Klinker Cope for the beautiful murals inside and outside the building, Ian Reid for amazing aerial photography, and Darren Williams, the Plantman for our foliage year-round. There are numerous others who we beg, borrow, and trade with, such as the Peony co-op; Charles, the Dahlia grower; Bear Creek Winery; and local farmers that provide fruits and veggies to juice, make soups, salads and smoothies.

With some purveyors we've had a long-term relationship — such as Captain's Coffee, Seafoods of Alaska, and Loopy Lupine Recycled Products — but we also encourage new start-ups, like Ohlson Mountain Mineral Springs H2O, and "Peonies on Pioneer."

In an industry known for high turnover, we're proud to have a core staff who have been with us for years, who enjoy the work, the challenge, and our place in the community. A lot of Homer's young people have worked with us over these years too, and we always look forward to their returning for summer employment as they mature into more responsible adults, learning the ropes, adapting to a fast pace, and taking pride in what they accomplish. They seem to have grown up quickly before our eyes, some even met and got married at Cosmic Kitchen, others return later with college degrees, children of their own, and fond memories of their time here.

We care about all the people we interact with — it's important to treat not just customers well but suppliers, employees, and anyone we do business with.

We believe good karma means you don't get away with anything and if you exceed expectations, people will always come back.

Bear Creek Winery

Here in Homer, Bear Creek Winery makes hand-crafted award-winning wines out of locally sourced berries, rhubarb and apples. Some of the more popular ones we serve at Cosmic Kitchen are Strawberry Rhubarb, Chardonnay, Shirazzberry, and Blueberry Mirlo. The winery also offers luxury guest rooms for B & B, including vouchers for breakfast at Cosmic Kitchen, just a short drive into town from Bear Creek Drive.

Stop in at their tasting room and visit with owners Dorothy and Bill Fry, and enjoy!

Brother Asaiah

We spent a number of years in Hawaii for the winter, returning to Homer for the summer seasons. One of those years we brought back a birthday gift for our friend, Brother Asaiah, an artist's interpretation, using coconut paper and wood block, titled "The Cosmic Spirit of Life". Unfortunately, Brother passed away the day before our return. So now this artwork hangs over the kitchen in his memory; see if you can spot it next time you're here.

The Plantman/Pastor & The Cartoonist

It's not exactly quiet living above the restaurant, but often at 7 a.m. we used to hear a vigorous scraping noise outside and wonder, "what is that?" Eventually, one of the doctors Michelle worked with joked about "turning her in" to Elderly Services for senior abuse, as he'd noticed her mom (Aileen) working on weeding the front of Cosmic Kitchen, down on her hands and knees, scraping away at the soil and arranging rocks into rows. Aileen was a habitual early riser and finished her work long before the morning staff arrived.

Needless to say, Michelle didn't inherit her mom's green thumb (nor the early rising gene!), so the plethora of summer planters on the deck and bonsai houseplants in the restaurant are courtesy of Darren Williams, aka The Plantman and the Pastor of the Refuge Chapel. His wife, Lorraine, is equally famous for her well-drawn, insightful cartoons depicting comical Homer scenarios.

We treasure this wonderful couple's cheerful contributions to our Cosmic lives.

Tony Meitler

The printer isn't working, the car won't start, the sinks are backing up! Who're you gonna call? Tony Meitler is who I call, as he always appears promptly in time of crisis, which seems to be just about every other day in the restaurant. As regular customers, Tony and his lovely wife, Carla, noticed me struggling to fix something one day and offered his services. As a retired Boeing engineer, he can put his hand to fixing anything, and I haven't lifted a tool since then. Almost every time he walked into the restaurant, I said, "just in time, Tony!" He soon thereafter named his new handyman service, "Just in Time Tony." Cosmic Kitchen would literally be in the dark without him (those six-foot neon bulbs are difficult to change!). Thanks, Tony.

133

BIG BANG SALSA BAR AND DIPS

CHIPOTLE SALSA

Chipotles are smoke-dried jalapeños and give fiery flavor to salsas and stews. These are easily obtained at the store in small 7-ounce cans and sold as "chipotle peppers in adobo sauce".

~ Makes 4½ Cups ~

1 (12-ounce can) crushed tomatoes
1 (7-ounce can) chipotle in adobe
1 teaspoon salt
1 teaspoon minced garlic
½ onion, diced
½ cup water
1 cup pineapple juice

Place all ingredients in a large bowl and blend with a hand blender for 1 minute (or in a food processor).

PINEAPPLE SALSA

This is another popular salsa to add to your Mexican fiesta. Some of our customers like it just as a 2-ounce "Shooter."

~ Makes 3 Cups ~

1 (14-ounce) can pineapple chunks
1 (12-ounce) can tomatillos
1 jalapeño (stem removed)
½ cup cilantro, chopped
¼ yellow onion
1 clove garlic
¼ cup water
1 teaspoon salt

Combine all ingredients in a food processor and puree until smooth, about 1 minute.

SALSA FRESCA

This mild salsa is a staple of Mexican Taquerias and one of our most widely used condiments. We use it in burritos, tacos, combos and our customers load up on it from the salsa bar where we call it "Homer Heat".

~ Makes 4 Cups ~

1 jalapeño chile pepper (stem removed)
2 medium tomatoes
1 cup water
½ teaspoon salt
2 cloves garlic
½ cup cilantro, chopped
1 (14.5-ounce) can crushed tomatoes
¼ yellow onion

1. In a 2 quart sauce pot, bring jalapeño, fresh tomatoes and water to a boil and simmer 2-3 minutes.
2. Combine the contents of the pot with the remaining ingredients in a food processor and puree until smooth.

Serve with warm tortilla chips.

ARBOL SALSA

Arbol chiles are easily found at the grocery store and are usually roasted to bring out the nutty flavor. They are spicy, but I also add a few Thai chiles to really pique the interest of those who like it hot!

~ Makes 4 Cups ~

1 cup Arbol chiles (stems removed)
2-3 dried Thai red chiles
½ cup canola oil
¼ yellow onion
2 Roma tomatoes, halved lengthwise
2 cups crushed tomatoes
1 (12-ounce) can tomatillos
1 clove garlic
½ teaspoon salt
⅓ cup cider vinegar

1. Lightly toast the chiles in a hot sauté pan with 1 tablespoon of oil, and then place them in a food processor.
2. In the same pan, sear the onion and Roma tomatoes until soft and charred around the edges.
3. Add them and the remaining ingredients to the processor and puree on high until smooth.

Serve with tacos, chips or any dish that needs a little zing!

SEAN'S CORN RELISH

We use corn relish in our salads, tacos and with chips as a dip. This recipe keeps it simple and fresh and lasts up to 5 days in the fridge.

~ Makes 3 Cups ~

1 red pepper, peeled and diced
2 tablespoons canola oil
½ cup red onion, diced
1 teaspoon garlic, chopped
2 cups corn (canned or frozen)
1 teaspoon mustard seed
1 teaspoon curry powder
1 lime (zest & juice)
3 tablespoons cilantro, chopped
salt and pepper to taste

1. Roast red pepper over an open flame until blackened, cool and peel.
2. Heat oil in a large frying pan, add onion, garlic, corn and diced red pepper and stir for about 5 minutes. Add in mustard seeds, curry powder and sauté a little longer.
3. Remove from heat, stir in the lime zest and juice, cilantro, salt and pepper. Mix well and serve or cover tightly and refrigerate for later use!

GUACAMOLE

Avocados are a smart choice in your daily options as the monosaturated fat is actually good for you. We use guacamole in BLTs, Mexican combo plates, burritos and as a starter with chips and salsa. Plan ahead as avocados are better purchased green or unripe. Place them in a paper bag for a day or two to ripen up; you should be able to press your thumb lightly into the avocado when it is ready to use.

~ Makes 2½ Cups ~

4 Haas avocados, scooped and pitted
2 tablespoons onion, diced
½ teaspoon garlic, chopped
1 tablespoon jalapeño chile, minced
2 tablespoons cilantro,
finely chopped
1½ teaspoons lime juice
1 teaspoon salt
½ teaspoon ground cumin
1 teaspoon jalapeño juice
¼ cup tomatoes, diced

Mix all ingredients except tomatoes, mashing to a chunky consistency, then add in tomatoes. Let set for at least 15 minutes to allow the flavors to come together.

Avocados will discolor, so if serving later, be sure to cover tightly, pressing plastic wrap against mixture to push out air, and refrigerate.

HUMMUS

Making Hummus is so easy and will raise your culinary skills to an impressive level. These beans are tasty and versatile, so you may want to keep extra in your pantry to add into soups and curries as well.

~ Makes 3 Cups ~

2 (15.5-ounce) cans garbanzo beans, drained
2 tablespoons chopped garlic
¼ cup lemon juice
1 teaspoon lemon zest
¼ teaspoon cayenne pepper
¼ teaspoon salt
2 tablespoons tahini paste
¾ cup olive oil

Place garbanzo beans in the food processor; add garlic, lemon, lemon zest, cayenne, salt and tahini paste. Turn on high setting and gradually add olive oil. Process until smooth.

Serve with warm pita bread or add to sandwiches for extra protein and flavor.

SUPERNOVA SPECIALS

COSMIC MEATLOAF

You always need a good recipe for meatloaf in your kitchen. It does require a little work, but it is worth it and most of the ingredients are already there in your pantry.

~ Makes enough for 6-8 ~

½ yellow onion
1 rib celery
½ green pepper
2 cloves garlic
5 tablespoons butter
½ teaspoon thyme, dried
½ teaspoon rosemary, ground
1 cup breadcrumbs
½ cup cream or half/half
2 pounds ground beef
½ pound pork sausage
⅓ cup ketchup
1 tablespoon Dijon mustard
3 large eggs, beaten
½ teaspoon Tabasco
2 tablespoons Worcestershire sauce
1 teaspoon salt
3 bacon strips
½ pound mushrooms

1. Preheat oven to 375° F and prep the veggies: chop the onion, celery and pepper into pea-sized pieces and mince the garlic.
2. Place 2 tablespoons of butter in a hot pan over medium heat and sauté the veggies, garlic, thyme and rosemary for 2 to 3 minutes.
3. Soak the breadcrumbs in the cream, then mix in a large bowl the meats, veggies, ketchup, mustard, eggs, Tabasco, Worcestershire, salt and breadcrumb mixture. Using your hands, combine everything thoroughly and form into an oval shape on a baking pan. Top with bacon strips and bake for 1 hour.
4. Meanwhile, slice the mushrooms and sauté them with 3 tablespoons of butter for 2 to 3 minutes.
5. After 1 hour, remove the bacon strips and bake the meatloaf for an additional 20 minutes. Remove from oven and allow to cool for a few minutes before serving.

Garnish with the cooked mushrooms and serve with mashed potatoes, of course (recipe follows).

MASHED POTATOES

4 pounds Yukon Gold or russet potatoes
1 tablespoon salt
1 cup milk
¾ cup (1½ sticks) butter
salt and white pepper to taste

1. Peel and cut the potatoes into 2-inch pieces; place them in a large pot with enough water to cover them by 1 inch. Add 1 tablespoon salt; bring to a boil and simmer for about 20-25 minutes, until tender.

2. Heat the milk and butter in a small sauce pot over medium heat until the butter is melted. Remove from heat.

3. Drain the potatoes, returning them to the pot and set it over low heat. Mash with a potato masher (or pass them through a ricer) and gradually add in the milk/butter mixture, stirring vigorously with a wooden spoon.

4. Season with salt and white pepper and serve with a few pats of butter on top.

MOUSSAKA

~ Makes enough for 12 ~

This Greek dish of layered potatoes, eggplant, beef and béchamel sauce rotated through the specials board during my time at Café Chanticleer in Point Loma, San Diego. Along with other classics such as Coq Au Vin, Veal Oscar, Salmon En Croute and Pork Au Poivre, I memorized a "galaxy" of European recipes that were never written down, just faithful to the taste buds of Chef Erik and me.

Sometimes you don't realize what a learning curve you're on, 'til later in life, from a distance, you gain perspective on treasured experiences.

I have no regrets except I would like more moussaka.

Moussaka:
2 pounds russet potatoes
2 medium eggplants
¼ cup flour
2 large eggs, beaten
3 tablespoons canola oil
2 pounds Maui-Wowee Ground
Beef, cooked (pg. 121)
1 tablespoon thyme
½ cup feta cheese
1½ cups tomato sauce

Béchamel Sauce:
2½ cups milk
¼ cup butter
½ cup flour
½ teaspoon salt
1 teaspoon nutmeg
2 eggs
Garnish: paprika

❖ ❖ ❖ ❖ ❖ ❖ ❖ ❖ ❖

1. Peel and slice the potatoes. Place them in a pan and cover with water, cook until just tender, 10 to 15 minutes, and drain.
2. Cut the ends off the eggplant, peel 3 or 4 strips of skin off and slice thinly into 1/4-inch rounds. Put ¼ cup flour in a large bowl and beat two eggs in another large bowl. Dredge the eggplant lightly in the flour and then in the eggs. In a hot pan with canola oil, fry the eggplant in batches until golden brown.
3. In a bowl mix the ground beef with thyme and the feta cheese.
4. For the béchamel sauce: first, in a medium sized pot, bring the milk to a boil. In a separate pan, melt the butter; add in ½ cup of flour stirring vigorously to form a roux. Gradually whisk the roux into the milk, reduce the heat, season with the salt and nutmeg, cooking for 5 to 10 minutes. Whisk the eggs, one at a time, continuously into the sauce and remove from heat.
5. In a 9 x 13 inch baking dish, spread the tomato sauce evenly. Then layer the potatoes, ground beef and eggplant on top. Pour the béchamel sauce evenly over the top; sprinkle with a little paprika. Bake at 375° for 45 minutes to 1 hour. Allow to cool a few minutes before serving.

THAI SALMON CAKES

The best salmon in the world is in Alaska. White Winter Kings and Sockeye salmon are my favorites. We have a lot of odd sounding seafood available here such as halibut cheeks, crab knuckles, black cod "batwings", dog salmon, chum salmon, Keta salmon, spotted shrimp and hundreds of species of rockfish.

At Cosmic Kitchen we have salmon filets delivered with the pin bones already removed, which is a nice convenience. We also get vacuum sealed packets of "spoon meat" scraped from the bones so it's less expensive and perfect to use in this recipe.

~ Makes 14 Cakes ~

¼ pound shrimp
2 pounds salmon
2 tablespoons mayonnaise
2 teaspoons red curry paste
2 large eggs
½ cup green onions
1 tablespoon red chili flakes
1 teaspoon salt
1 teaspoon sugar
2 teaspoons cornstarch
1½ cups panko breadcrumbs
3 tablespoons canola oil
Thai sweet chili sauce
1 tablespoon cilantro, chopped

1. Peel and devein the shrimp, remove the skin and pin bones from the salmon and chop into large pieces. In a food processor, pulse the shrimp and salmon together into a pea-sized consistency.
2. In a large bowl, whisk together the mayo, curry paste, eggs, green onion, chili flakes, salt, sugar and cornstarch. Combine the shrimp/salmon into this until thoroughly mixed.
3. Scoop 1/3-cup-size patties into the panko, coating both sides, forming about 14 cakes, and place onto a platter; refrigerate for 30 minutes.
4. Heat the oil in a large pan and fry the cakes in batches until golden brown, about 3 to 4 minutes per side.

Drizzle with Thai sweet chili sauce and cilantro.

ROPA VIEJA

This signature dish of Cuba is infused with Latin American flavors. Traditionally made with beef, I "Hawaiianized" the recipe with pork shoulder. The initial braising of the pork is a convenient twist in preparing "Kalua pig" (you don't have to roast it in an underground stone oven for 8 hours!). An excellent recipe itself in case you need to bring a potluck dish to a luau.

~ Makes mucho pork ~

Braised Pork:
3 pounds pork shoulder
4 whole garlic cloves
½ yellow onion, sliced
2 bay leaves
1 tablespoon salt
1 tablespoon liquid smoke

Ropa Vieja:
2 tablespoons canola oil
2 cups Fajita Veggies (pg. 115)
1 tablespoon cumin
1 tablespoon thyme
½ cup white wine
½ cup tomato paste
2 cups crushed tomato
2 cups broth (from cooked pork)
2 tablespoons capers
½ cup sliced green olives

Garnish: cilantro

1. Cut the pork into large, 4-inch, pieces. Place them in a large soup pot with the garlic, onion, bay leaf, salt and liquid smoke; fill with water to cover everything by about 1 inch. Bring to a boil and simmer until tender, about 1½ hours.
2. Remove the pork to a platter and shred with 2 forks, or your fingers if cool enough. Reserve the strained broth for later.
3. In a large pot, heat the canola oil, sauté the Fajita Veggies with the cumin and thyme, then deglaze with the wine. Add the tomato paste, crushed tomatoes, 2 cups broth and shredded pork. Simmer for 15-20 minutes, stirring regularly to avoid scorching the bottom. Stir in the capers and olives and garnish with cilantro.

We serve this special with black beans, rice and corn tortillas.

CHICKEN ADOBO

~ Makes enough for 4 ~

1 cup rice vinegar
2 cups soy sauce
2 tablespoons garlic, minced
1 (2-inch high) "knob" ginger, smashed
2 bay leaves
1 yellow onion, large dice
1 cup pineapple juice
1 teaspoon black peppercorns
1 cup Sprite soda
4 each chicken legs and thighs
1¼ cups water
3 tablespoons canola oil
½ cup cornstarch

Living in Hawaii for years, I worked with many Filipinos and came to love their national dish when served as the employee meal. Sometimes I created the daily soup out of leftover chicken adobo with the addition of onions, potatoes and carrots. Nothing goes to waste in the kitchen of a French chef, particularly if he has Irish roots, worked in Hawaii and is making Filipino food.
Bon Appétit!

1. In a large soup pot, combine the vinegar, soy sauce, garlic, ginger, bay leaves, onion, pineapple juice, peppercorns and Sprite together with the chicken. Allow to marinate at least 30 minutes.
2. Add 1 cup of water to the pot, bring to a boil, and then simmer for 45 minutes.
3. Remove the chicken with a slotted spoon to a platter and pat dry with paper towels. Discard the knob of ginger but save the marinade. In a wok or sauté pan, heat the oil until hot and sear the chicken until brown on all sides, 5 to 6 minutes.
4. Dissolve the cornstarch in ¼ cup of water. Reheat the marinade, adding in the cornstarch and stirring constantly to form a smooth sauce. Return the chicken to the pot and simmer for a few more minutes.

Serve with steamed rice.

CHICKEN TIKKA MASALA CURRY

We've lived in the apartment above the business since it opened in 2003 and have gotten used to the daily sounds of the restaurant, the shuffling noise of chairs downstairs, delivery trucks coming and going and the laughter of customers in the background.

Our commute to work is great, especially in winter, but gradually Michelle noticed something missing in the upstairs kitchen. On Valentine's Day she couldn't find her candle holders; around the holidays her favorite pots and dishes were nowhere to be found. Finally she realized that when the restaurant caters events, things disappear! So now there's a cabinet dedicated to catering supplies only.

Chicken Tikka Masala has become a staple of the Cosmic "specials menu" and deserves your best table settings (and Michelle's).

~ Makes enough for 4-6 ~

4 Chicken Tikka, cubed (pg. 33)
2 cups Fajita Veggies (pg. 115)
1 tablespoon canola oil
2 cloves garlic, minced
1 inch fresh ginger, minced
1 tablespoon Tikka Spice (pg. 33)
1 teaspoon garam masala
1 cup vegetable broth
¼ cup heavy cream
1 cup plain yogurt
1 teaspoon sugar

1. Prep the Chicken Tikka and the Fajita Veggies.
2. Heat the oil in a large pot over medium heat, sauté the Fajita Veggies and add in the garlic, ginger and dry spices, stirring as they become fragrant.
3. Stir in the chicken, broth, and heavy cream and simmer for 15 minutes.
4. Add in the yogurt and sugar; turn off the heat and stir gently.

Serve with jasmine rice and chutney.

COCONUT AND WASABI CRUSTED SALMON
with Sesame Salad

This Hawaii/Alaska fusion dish brings the best of the two states together. The crust keeps the fish moist on the inside, with a burst of heat from the wasabi and crunch from the toasted coconut — who needs boring old fish 'n chips?

~ Makes 4 servings ~

4 (6-ounce) salmon filets
salt and pepper to taste
½ teaspoon oregano
2 teaspoons lime juice
4 teaspoons wasabi paste
1 cup shredded coconut
1 cup panko
2 tablespoons canola oil
sweet chili sauce

Sesame Salad:
½ cup rice wine vinegar
¼ cup honey
¼ cup soy sauce
3 tablespoons sriracha sauce
1 cup peanut oil
¼ cup sesame oil
1 bag mixed greens

Garnish: avocado and Marinated Cucumbers (pg. 58)

1. Preheat the oven to 375° F. Season the fish with salt, pepper, oregano and lime juice. Place the filets skin side down on a plate and smear 1 teaspoon of wasabi evenly over the top of each filet.
2. Mix the coconut and panko together and press into the wasabi-coated fish to form a crust on 1 side only.
3. In a hot skillet, place the salmon crusted side down into the sizzling oil for 2 to 3 minutes. Turn the fish over and finish in the oven.
4. For the dressing: Place the vinegar, honey, soy sauce and sriracha in a bowl and slowly whisk in the peanut and sesame oil. Toss the mixed greens with just enough dressing to coat the leaves. Garnish with avocado and Marinated Cucumber.
5. Drizzle the salmon with sweet chili sauce and serve with the sesame-dressed salad and short grain rice.

TEQUILA SHRIMP AND SCALLOP FETTUCCINE

I must confess that I've worked in more Italian restaurants than Mexican. My first job in the U.S. was as a bartender in an Italian restaurant in Provincetown, Massachusetts. The longest job I held was sous-chef at Carmine's Trattoria for 3 years in West Palm Beach, Florida, but my most memorable one was at Club Colette in the upscale town of neighboring Palm Beach. An eclectic private club with French waiters, a motley kitchen crew (Portuguese, Moroccan and Irish) owned by a Brazilian dandy and serving the richest of the rich "Art-Culinaire" style Italian food.

I broiled the veal chops, swordfish and escargot served alongside fabulous pastas of tagliatelle with truffles and penne with shitake mushrooms. Desserts were flambé "this", soufflé "that" accompanied with miniature chocolate "grand pianos". The well-healed clientele had their limos, Caddies and Rolls Royces valet parked up and down the street (my old Ford truck was the only one around for miles).

It was there I began to realize my disdain for the "Downton Abbey" style of restaurant, my Irish Republican blood felt that service, food and nutrition needn't be sacrificed at more egalitarian establishments. There is no valet service at Cosmic Kitchen and most of the vehicles in the parking lot are trucks anyway. We pool the tips equally among all the staff, a new trend that we've been doing all along. Our service is interactive – you order at the counter and we serve you the food, promptly.

Quite often I crave pasta and this Tequila Scallop and Shrimp Fettuccine satisfies that need with its buttery, garlic cream, Alaska seafood and a hint of tequila. You could even call it gourmet, just don't say it too loudly at the Cosmic Kitchen.

~ Makes enough for 4 ~

Continued on next page…

3 tablespoons roasted garlic puree
12 ounces fettuccine pasta
2 tablespoons canola oil
12 ounces shrimp, peeled and deveined
12 scallops
1½ cups Fajita Veggies (pg. 115)
¼ cup tequila
1½ cups heavy cream
2 tablespoons butter
salt and pepper to taste

Garnish: garlic bread, cilantro, lime wedges

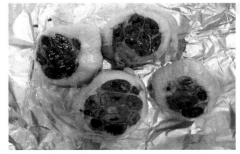

Roasted Garlic Puree

4 whole heads of garlic
1 teaspoon olive oil

1. Prepare the roasted garlic (recipe follows).
2. Cook the pasta according to the package directions.
3. Heat the oil in a large fry pan until very hot, add the shrimp and scallops and sauté for 3 to 4 minutes, and then slide them onto a plate.
4. Continue in the same hot pan, sauté the Fajita Veggies for a couple of minutes, stir in the garlic puree and deglaze with the tequila. As it flames up, pour in the heavy cream, butter, shrimp, scallops and stir well.
5. Simmer for 5 to 10 minutes, add in the cooked fettuccine with 2 to 3 tablespoons of the pasta water to thin out the sauce if you prefer, season with salt and pepper.
6. Using tongs, mound the pasta into bowls and divide the sea-food and sauce among them. Serve with toasted garlic bread, cilantro and lime.

1. Heat the oven to 400° F.
2. Cut ¼ inch off the garlic tops and place them cut side down on a sheet of foil. Drizzle the oil over the top and wrap them in foil.
3. Roast the garlic on a baking tray in the oven for about 1 hour. Allow to cool, then squeeze the cloves out of the skins and mash them in a bowl.

PLANET DESSERT

GINGER-CHOCOLATE CHIP COOKIES

This great combination of ginger and chocolate might give the Girl Scouts some competition. We can't keep enough of these babies on the counter, so now you can make your own batch. But please come in and see us anyway – we would miss you!

~ Makes 10 Cookies ~

2 cups all-purpose flour
1 cup chocolate chips
2 teaspoons baking soda
½ teaspoon salt
1½ teaspoons cinnamon
1 teaspoon ground ginger
¾ teaspoon ground cardamom
½ cup (1 stick) unsalted butter, softened at room temperature
½ cup granulated sugar
1 large egg
⅓ cup molasses
¼ cup granulated sugar (for rolling cookies in)

1. Pre-heat the oven to 425° F.
2. In a small bowl, whisk together the flour, chocolate chips, baking soda, salt and spices.
3. In a medium bowl (or electric mixer with a paddle) beat together the butter, sugar, egg and molasses, then add in the dry ingredients slowly, mixing it all together.
4. Scoop the dough into 10 balls, about golf ball size, and roll in the granulated sugar. Place on parchment paper lined baking pans and refrigerate for 20 minutes.
5. Bake for 15-20 minutes until cookies puff up and are just set around the edges.

CHOCOLATE BROWNIES

~ Makes 24 Brownies ~

1 pound unsalted butter
1 pound and 12 ounces semi-sweet chocolate chips
6 ounces bitter chocolate
6 large eggs
3 tablespoons instant coffee
2 tablespoons vanilla
2¼ cups sugar
1 teaspoon salt
1 tablespoon baking powder
1¼ cup flour
3 cups walnuts, chopped

This recipe is from the Natural Food Store on Pioneer Avenue where I worked for a couple of years. I helped in its remodel from an old hippie store into a modern deli/café but it didn't survive the changing times, and closed some years later. It's been said that success is never final and failure is only temporary, and I keep that in mind as I believe grit and perseverance are necessary to succeed at anything.

So if you've never made a really great brownie, here is a recipe to demonstrate your perseverance in learning a new skill – welcome to Bakery 101.

1. Preheat oven to 345° F. Butter and flour a 9 x 13 inch baking dish.
2. Melt together butter, 1 pound of chocolate chips, and bitter chocolate in a double boiler (a bowl set over a pot of gently boiling water).
3. In a separate bowl stir together eggs, coffee, vanilla and sugar. Stir chocolate mixture into eggs and allow to cool.
4. Mix salt, baking powder, and 1 cup of flour together and add to cooled mixture.
5. Mix walnuts, ¼ cup flour, and 12 ounces of chips. Add to mixture.
6. Spread mixture evenly in the pan and bake for 40 minutes. Test sides and back. Rotate and cook for 15 more minutes if needed.

174

WHITE CHOCOLATE AND MACADAMIA NUT COOKIES

Another Hawaiian inspired treat, with crunchy, buttery macadamia nuts pairing well with white chocolate chips.

~ Makes 12 Cookies ~

2 cups all-purpose flour
1 cup quick cooking or old fashioned oats
1 teaspoon baking powder
1 teaspoon baking soda
1 teaspoon salt
10 ounces (2½ sticks) unsalted butter, at room temperature
1 cup brown sugar
½ cup granulated sugar
2 eggs, at room temperature
1 tablespoon vanilla extract
1½ cups white chocolate chips
1½ cups macadamia nuts (crushed in blender into small pieces)

1. Preheat oven to 350° F. Line 2 baking sheets with parchment paper.
2. In a medium bowl, mix the flour with the oats, baking powder, baking soda and salt. In a standing mixer fitted with a paddle, beat the butter with both sugars at medium speed until creamy. Add 1 whole egg, plus 1 egg yolk, and the vanilla, and continue beating for 1-2 minutes.
3. Add in remaining ingredients and mix well.
4. Scoop heaping teaspoons of the dough onto the baking sheet about 2 inches apart, and bake for 15-20 minutes. Allow to cool and transfer to a platter. They may be stored in an airtight container, or frozen for later use.

MEXICAN FLAN

Caramel Custard is a staple of Mexican restaurants. It's easy and can be made ahead of time, and then just plated up for a simply delicious dessert.

~ Makes 6-8 Flans ~

2 tablespoons fresh orange juice
orange zest
1¾ cups sugar
3¼ cups milk
2 teaspoons vanilla extract
6 whole eggs

1. Preheat oven to 350° F.
2. Zest the orange and chop it lightly, squeeze the juice into a cup.
3. Combine 1 cup of sugar and orange juice in a small saucepan. Bring to a boil over high heat, stirring continuously with a metal spoon, and continue cooking until a dark caramel color is reached. Remove from heat and quickly pour the caramel into 6-8 ceramic soup cups.
4. For the custard, whisk ¾ cups sugar, orange zest, milk, vanilla, and eggs in a bowl for 2-3 minutes. Divide this mixture among the cups with the caramel.
5. Place the cups in a large baking dish filled with 2-3 inches of hot water. Bake for approximately 1 hour until the custard is set but a little wiggly in the center. Remove from oven and allow to cool. Refrigerate flans until ready to serve.
6. Run a sharp knife around the edges of each flan, and invert onto a 6-inch serving plate, tapping lightly to pop the flan out. Serve with whipped cream.

SMOOTHIES

At last, a smoothie menu we can all agree on (or not). Smoothies are easy to make and are best made with frozen fruit such as bananas, peaches, and mangos, cut into one-inch pieces for that creamy, thick consistency. Freeze the cut fresh fruit on a plate, then slide it into ziplock bags for future use.

Wild Berry Elixir
2 cups wild berries
1 tablespoon plain yogurt
3-4 mint leaves
1 cup apple juice

Blend until smooth.

Peach Fuzzy Navel
2 cups frozen peaches
2 tablespoon plain yogurt
½ cup mango nectar
½ cup apple juice

Blend until smooth.

Strawberry Banana
1 cup frozen strawberries
1 cup frozen bananas
1 cup apple juice

Blend until smooth.

Mango Madness
2 cups frozen mango
½ cup mango nectar
1 cup apple juice

Blend until smooth.

FRESH JUICES

Juices are a nutritious and refreshing way to start the day. Juicing removes the fiber so it speeds up absorption into your body of all the ingredients of fruit and veggies. Add a piece of fresh ginger or squeeze of lime for extra zing. We often combine the fresh juice with frozen fruit for our hybrids of delicious Juice/Smoothie combos, such as the Revitalizer and Energizer drinks.

If you plan on juicing a lot, pick up an inexpensive centrifugal juicer for less than $100. It's a fun and healthy investment that will surprise you with its versatility.

"Both life and love are like butter and do not keep: they both have to be made fresh every day."

Marge Piercy

Tropical Revitalizer
1 apple
1 peeled orange
1" piece of ginger
1 carrot
2 cups frozen mango
½ cup mango nectar

Put the apple, orange, carrot and ginger through the juicer, then blend this juice with the mango and nectar.

Wild Berry Energizer
2 apples
1 peeled orange
1" piece of ginger
1 cup frozen wild berries
1 tablespoon plain yogurt
3-4 mint leaves

Put the apples, orange and ginger through the juicer, then puree this juice in a blender with the frozen berries, yogurt and mint.

> For each juice recipe, put all ingredients through the juicer, alternating between leafy greens and juicy fruit to keep everything moving.

Green Power
3 cups spinach
1 medium carrot
2 apples
1 peeled orange
½ peeled lemon
1" piece of ginger
½ cup cilantro

Cosmic Sunrise
2 medium carrots
2 apples
1 peeled orange
½ peeled lemon
1" piece of ginger

Cosmic Sunset
2 medium beets
1 medium carrot
2 apples
1 peeled orange
½ peeled lemon
1" piece of ginger

ACT II – IF YOU BUILD IT...

510 E Pioneer Avenue had a checkered history before Cosmic Kitchen – it was a B&B, a kitchen supply store, and an artist's pottery shop and loft. People seemed relieved actually, that it finally found a meaningful purpose after its eclectic earlier life. It was originally built by Lynn Wolf, an artist from California, who kindly made us a scrapbook of her pioneering style of construction – fearless innocence with a dash of American "can-do" spirit. I guess we inherited her chutzpah.

Another wonderful pioneering lady came into ownership of the building, Amy Springer, who also generously helped us envision our dream by enlarging the parking lot and refurbishing the upstairs loft into a livable space. We eventually bought the property from Amy.

I helped with the remodeling upstairs while we waited for the pottery shop lease to run out downstairs. We got possession of the whole building on April 1, 2003 and set about constructing the restaurant with a goal of one month to opening day. Demolition is the easy part that I learned from assisting the work crew while observing the pride of workmanship in each trade. The carpenters, electricians, plumbers, painters, tilers, and many others set about their

tasks with professionalism that I still admire, and all of them are still regular customers, despite my frantic pacing and incessant questions of "how much longer?".

It was an exhilarating and hectic time as we quickly learned the jargon needed to understand the various professions we came in contact with: banking/finance, health department, fire department, city hall/planning department, alcohol licensing, etc. and, of course, restaurant equipment, refrigeration, furniture, staffing, advertising and menu printing.

Amazingly, everything went according to plan, we got approved for a bank loan and the business plan fell into place. The construction crew worked

together in a pas de deux (or more) taking turns in finishing their specialty. If you've ever built your own home, you'll understand the chaos.

The paint color that we painstakingly chose dried overnight to a sickening shade of orange, but we convinced ourselves it's OK and will mellow into the promised "copper glaze." The kitchen staff prepped all week and we opened on May 1, 2003 (Mayday – a distress call we thought appropriate, but actually it's our anniversary also). The first day we prepared lunch as a thank-you to all the tradesmen and others who helped us get this far. The second day we opened to the public, who confirmed we were on the right track with good food, good service and good prices.

Thanks to the Cosmic Hamlet of Homer supporting us throughout the years, our hardworking staff, Michelle's good karma and my dogged determination, the first ten years flew by. We can hardly believe such good fortune happening to a pair of travel-happy hippies like us. Well into our second act now, we know we can't be all things to everybody, but will continue to strive to keep the Cosmic Kitchen in tune with the wonderful community we landed in.

THANKS!

We owe a world of thanks to all the cast and crew that have made the restaurant and this book possible.

We can hardly thank Leah Tufares enough. She's been with us since the beginning, and is wonderfully professional, a joy to customers, and a pleasure to work with; she always has a positive outlook. Her true grit is exemplary to all of us.

Thanks to the crew whose daily efforts contribute to the good vibe of this crazy kitchen, especially Danielle and Jonathan who have been with us a long time, and all the others now and throughout the years — Debbie, Tori, Eliott, Cruz, Jessica, Rose (& her great artwork), Bob (& his fun sculptures) — and all the rest. Thank you all!

Many thanks to our editor, Jan O'Meara for taking on this project. Her patience and attention to detail seem miraculous in our case. And to the photographers who made the food look as good as it truly is!

We can't forget to thank our suppliers who work hard to provide us with consistent, high quality products that keep this show on the road.

We are especially indebted to the people of this cosmic hamlet of Homer (and beyond!) whose love and support have made Cosmic Kitchen possible.

And of course to my wife, Michelle, who takes care of the behind the scenes work, including bookkeeping, payroll, and attending to all the little details that would otherwise be missed, including the formatting of this book. She has been my cheerleader, confidant, and soul mate in all endeavors.

INDEX

BIOGRAPHY

Sean Hogan was born and raised in Dublin, Ireland, moved to the U.S. in the mid-eighties where he met and fell in love with Michelle Wilson, a Minnesota girl working as an RN in Phoenix, Arizona.

Sean graduated from Florida Culinary Institute, served a chef apprenticeship in Zurich, Switzerland, participating in ACF cooking competitions with honors and medals for statewide events.

Michelle continued her career in dialysis nursing as Sean racked up experience as chef-de-cuisine in various restaurants and hotels as their love of travel, and adventures together, brought them from Florida to Hawaii, Switzerland and back again to the U.S.

Eventually, they visited Alaska to see Michelle's parents, who spent their summers on the Kenai Peninsula. They opened Cosmic Kitchen on May 1st 2003, in the quaint little building on Pioneer Avenue in the middle of Homer, Alaska. It was a popular restaurant from the beginning, with locals and visitors alike appreciating the great food, great menu, and friendly atmosphere of the Cosmic Kitchen.